CONTENTS

CONTENTS

BEFORE YOU START...

Sometimes you will find numbers in the text, either at the beginning of a line or after a word.

These numbers correspond to drawings and diagrams, usually placed below the text.

EXAMPLE:
Number at the beginning of the line:
1.   Cartilage, which covers the friction surfaces of bones.

Number after a word:
Tendons (2) attach muscles to bones.

To find out where the cartilage is, you need to look at number 1 on the drawing. To find out where the tendon is, look at number 2.

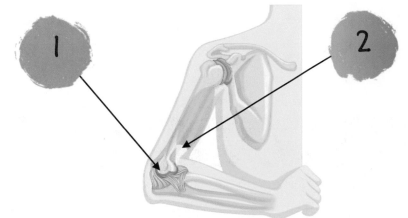

Other times you will find drawings and diagrams with colors. Each color placed in a small circle corresponds to the same color in the diagram.

EXAMPLE:
In the diagram below, the frontal lobe is the part colored yellow on the drawing of the brain.

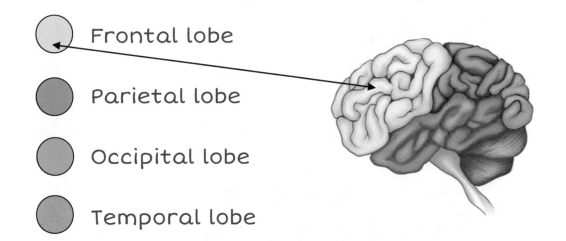

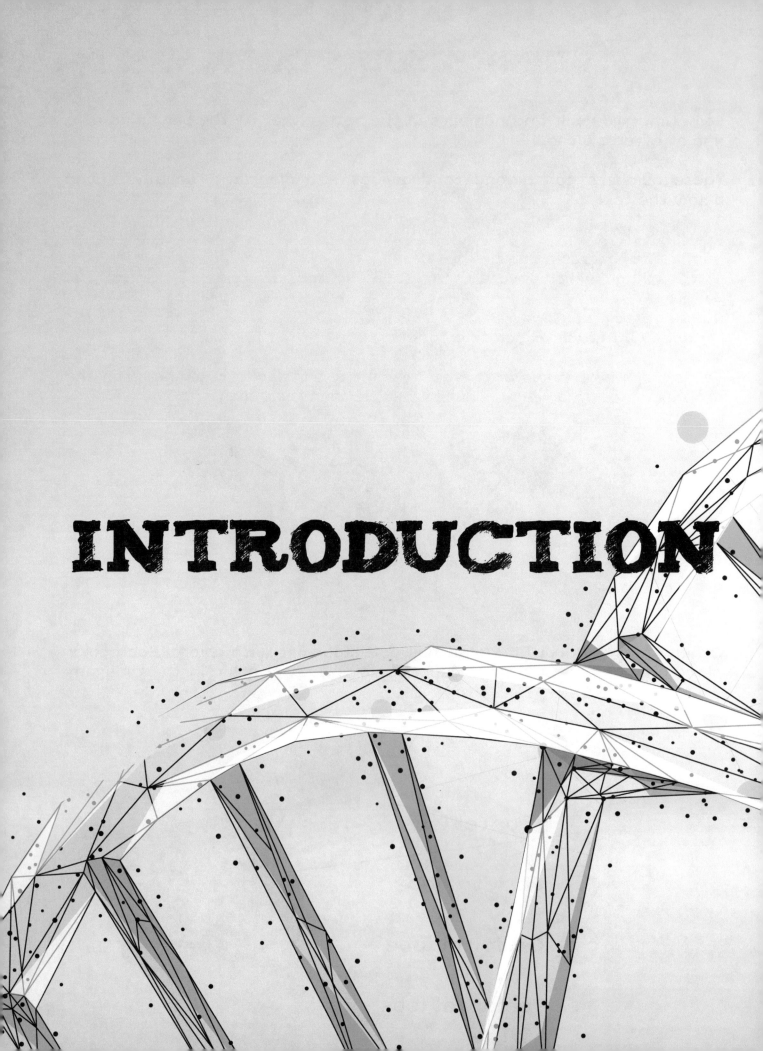

INTRODUCTION

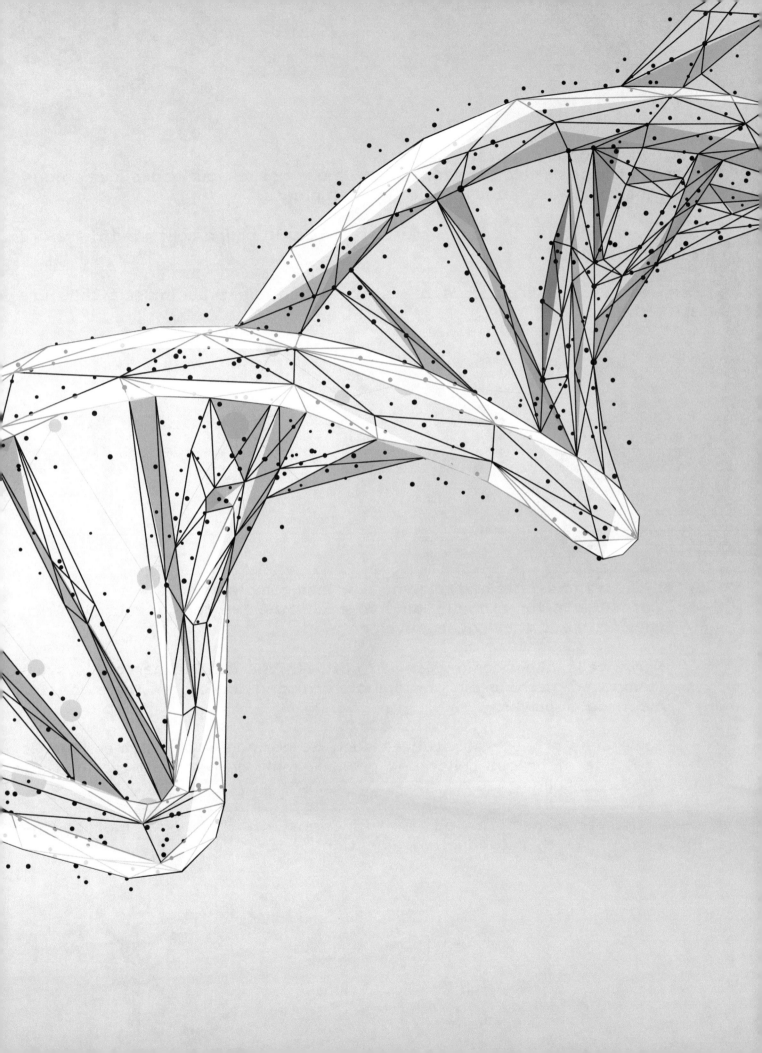

THE CELLS

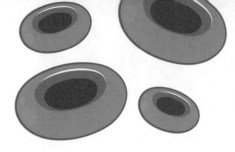

Our body is made of cells.
A cell is the basic element that makes up our tissues, our bones, our organs. All living things are made up of cells, even plants.

In the human body, there are more than 50,000 billion cells, and there are 300 different kinds.

For example, our brain cells are star-shaped, while our muscle cells are stick-shaped.

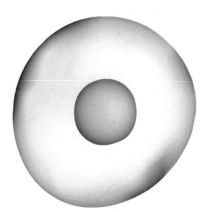

A cell always has a defined role, more or less complex.

- Muscle cells, for example, bind to each other to form a muscle. When they contract, they cause movement.

- Nerve cells allow communication between the central nervous system (composed of the brain and spinal cord) and the organs, by means of electrical impulses.

- Some cells produce substances such as hormones or enzymes. This is the case of breast cells that produce milk, or pancreatic cells that produce insulin.

Cells therefore perform all the functions of the body: metabolism, movement, growth, reproduction, digestion...

A cell is made up of several components:

- The membrane (1) is an envelope (or skin) called the plasma membrane. This membrane contains the cytoplasm and the nucleus.

- The cytoplasm (2) contains many biomolecules, such as proteins, and organelles (which are cellular structures), such as mitochondria (3), which provide energy for the cell to function.

- The nucleus (4) contains most of the cell's genetic material.

It is also important to know that a cell contains water.

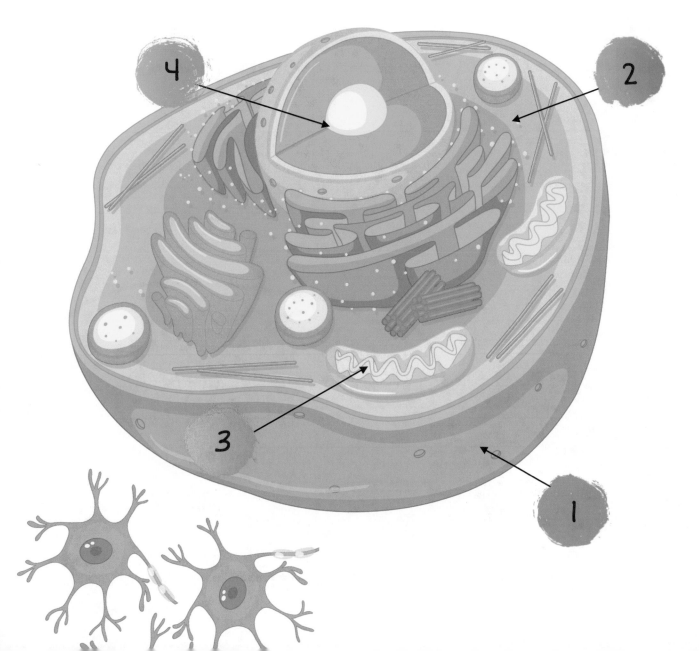

This genetic material, also called the genome, is distributed in 46 chromosomes (23 pairs). For each pair, there is a chromosome of paternal origin, and a chromosome of maternal origin.

Chromosomes are made up of DNA. A DNA molecule contains the genetic code, which is all the information necessary for the development and functioning of the body (a bit like a construction plan). DNA looks like two ribbons wound in a helix.

A gene is a piece of DNA that corresponds to a specific piece of genetic information. For example, it is a specific gene that defines the color of our eyes, or our hair, or determines our height.

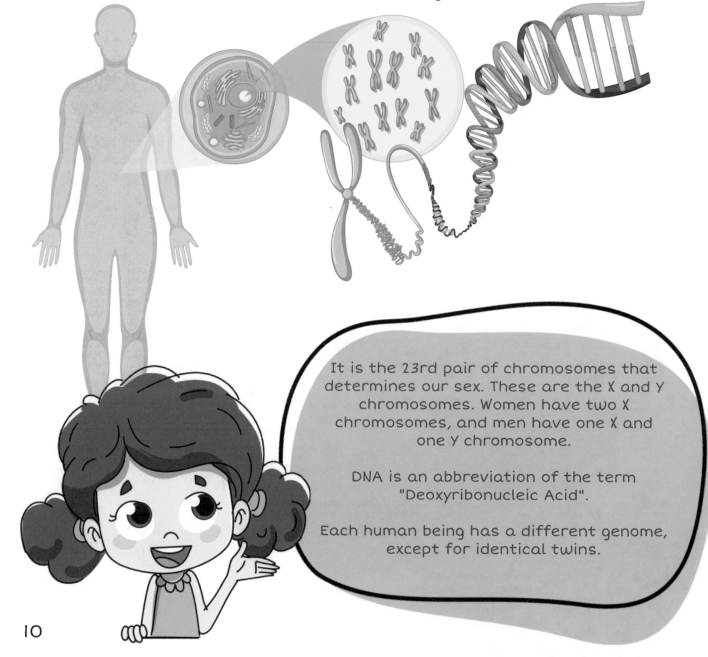

It is the 23rd pair of chromosomes that determines our sex. These are the X and Y chromosomes. Women have two X chromosomes, and men have one X and one Y chromosome.

DNA is an abbreviation of the term "Deoxyribonucleic Acid".

Each human being has a different genome, except for identical twins.

THE WATER

The human body contains a lot of water. The quantity of water in an adult represents on average 65% of its weight.

This amount can vary depending on age and body size:
- The thinner a person is, the greater the proportion of water in their body. Fat has a very low water content.
- The older a person is, the faster the body tends to dehydrate.
- At birth, a baby's body is about 80% water.

The body does not store water. It constantly eliminates water through urine, breathing and perspiration. It is therefore very important to drink regularly.

Most of the water in the body is found in the cells, in varying amounts depending on the type of cell:
- Blood cells contain about 85% water.
- Brain, lung and muscle cells contain about 75% water.
- Bone cells contain 20% water.
- Adipose tissue (fat) contains only 10% water.

Water is therefore a very important component of our body, and participates in several essential functions:
- Water is involved in maintaining a constant temperature inside the body, through perspiration. When we are hot, the sweat glands (located in the skin) retain some of the water in the bloodstream and then eliminate it through perspiration. This process allows the body to cool down.
- During digestion, the body supplies water to the stomach and small intestine to facilitate the circulation and digestion of food. At the end of the digestion process, a large part of this water passes through the intestinal walls into the bloodstream.
- Water facilitates the elimination of waste.
- Water is involved in many chemical reactions in the body, and participates in the transport of these substances in the body.
- Water participates in the elasticity of certain tissues such as the skin and lubricates certain organs such as the eye.

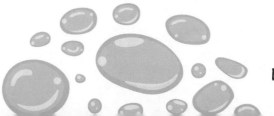

THE SKELETON AND MUSCLES

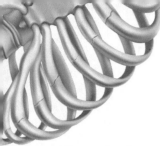

THE SKELETON

The skeleton is the set of bones in the human body.

The skeleton has several roles:
- To support the weight of the body, and allow its mobility (thanks to the muscles which are attached to the bones).
- Protect organs: The skull protects the brain, the rib cage protects the heart and lungs...
- Store reserves: Bones contain 99% of the body's calcium and phosphorus reserves.
- Blood production: Bones are where red and white blood cells, as well as platelets, are produced, thanks to the bone marrow.

The skeleton is made up of 206 bones, most of which are connected by joints.

Generally, we distinguish the cephalic skeleton (i.e. the skull), the axial skeleton (composed of the thoracic cage - ribs and sternum - and the vertebral column) and the appendicular skeleton (i.e. the limbs).

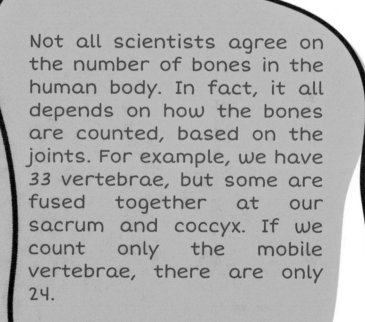

Not all scientists agree on the number of bones in the human body. In fact, it all depends on how the bones are counted, based on the joints. For example, we have 33 vertebrae, but some are fused together at our sacrum and coccyx. If we count only the mobile vertebrae, there are only 24.

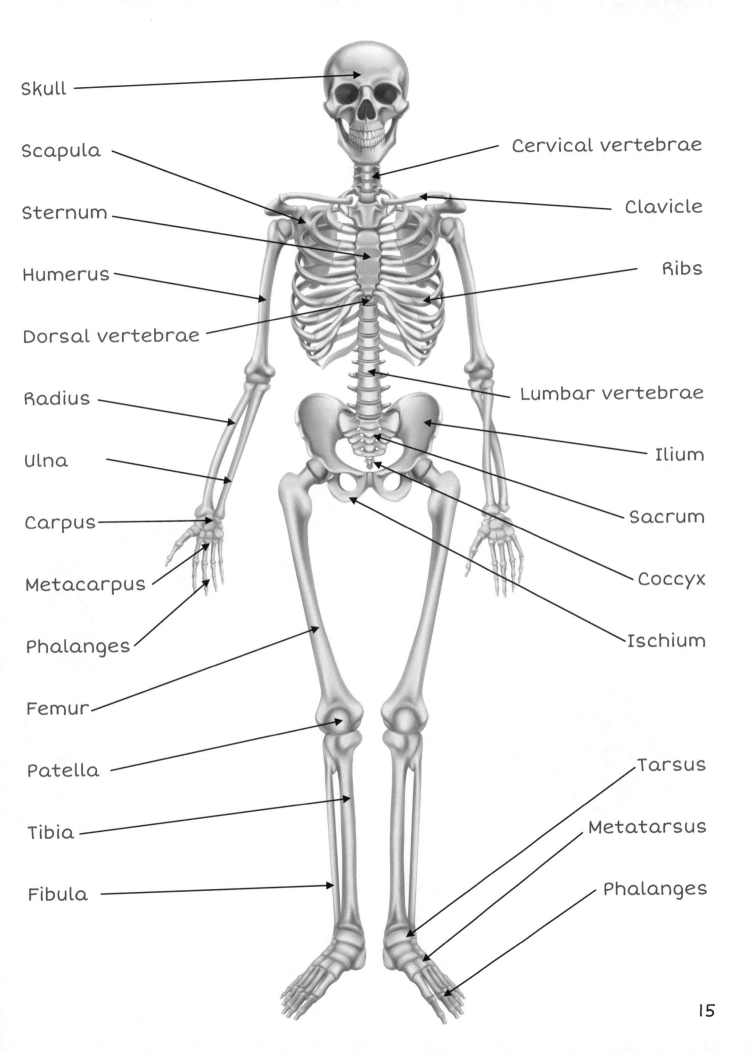

Skull

Scapula

Sternum

Humerus

Dorsal vertebrae

Radius

Ulna

Carpus

Metacarpus

Phalanges

Femur

Patella

Tibia

Fibula

Cervical vertebrae

Clavicle

Ribs

Lumbar vertebrae

Ilium

Sacrum

Coccyx

Ischium

Tarsus

Metatarsus

Phalanges

15

THE SKULL

The skull is the set of bones that make up our head.

The skull is connected to the spine by the first cervical vertebra, also called Atlas.

The skull is composed of several bones (22 in total), which are mostly fused together.

The main role of the skull is to protect our brain, but also other organs. The eyes, for example, are partly protected by the orbits, the inner part of our ears is also protected by the skull. Our nasal cavities, which are the seat of our sense of smell, are also in our skull.
Many muscles are also attached to the different bones, such as the facial muscles, which allow our facial expressions (smile for example).
Finally, the skull has a role of resonance when we speak or sing.

When a baby is born, the bones of the skull are not yet fused together, creating gaps.
These gaps, called fontanelles, are mainly located on the top of the skull, between the parietal bones, the frontal bone, and the occipital bone.
The baby's skull is therefore soft. This facilitates the passage of the head during delivery, but also the growth of the brain.
Generally, these bones are completely fused by the age of 18 months.

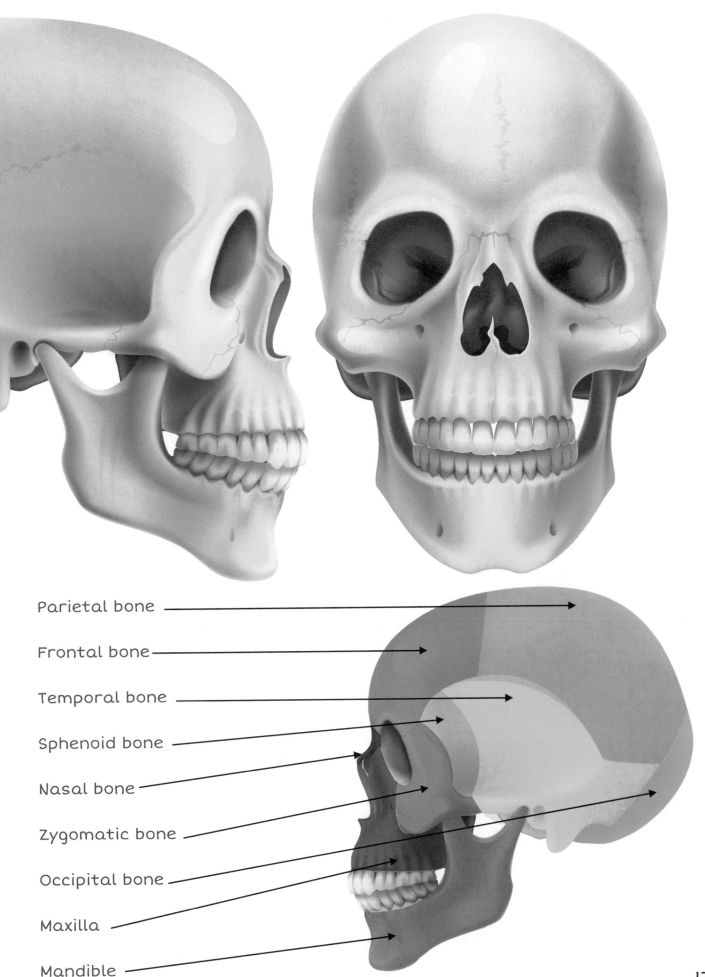

Parietal bone

Frontal bone

Temporal bone

Sphenoid bone

Nasal bone

Zygomatic bone

Occipital bone

Maxilla

Mandible

17

THE BONES

A bone is composed of two distinct parts:
• A mineral part, made of calcium, fluorine, iron and other trace elements.
• An organic part, composed of proteins, bone cells, and water.

A bone is composed of several elements:
1. The compact bone (the hard and white part of the bone, largely mineral)
2. The spongy bone, in which the bone marrow is located (also called red marrow).
3. Articular cartilage, which covers the ends of the bones
4. Yellow marrow, which is found in most long bones (such as the femur), and is a fatty mass.
5. Blood vessels: Tiny arteries and veins bring nutrients and oxygen to the bones.

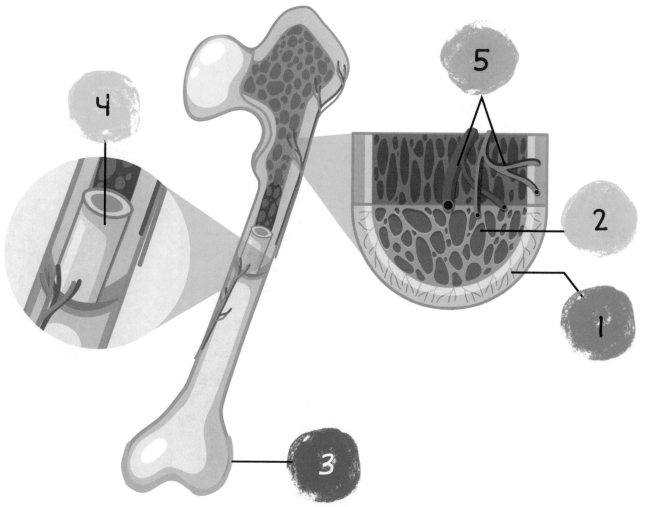

THE CARTILAGE

Cartilage is an organic tissue that is both flexible and resistant, sometimes elastic.

It is sometimes confused with bone, but it is not bone. Cartilage is essentially composed of a protein called collagen.

In the human body, there are 3 types of cartilage:
- Hyaline cartilage: This is the cartilage that covers the end of the bones at the joints, but also our nasal septum. This cartilage constitutes the skeleton of the embryo. Generally, the hyaline cartilage is lubricated by a liquid. This liquid, the synovium, covers the articular surfaces. Thus, the cartilage allows to reduce the friction of the bones and facilitates the mobility of the articulations. It also helps to absorb shocks and tensions.

- Fibrous cartilage: This cartilage constitutes for example the intervertebral discs, the menisci (knee cartilage), or the insertions of ligaments and tendons on the bones. This cartilage is very resistant.

- Elastic cartilage: This is the cartilage that makes up our ears, or certain parts of our larynx.

Unlike our bones, cartilage does not regenerate.
With age, or following an accident, cartilage wears out and causes inflammation, such as arthrosis or arthritis.

THE JOINTS

A joint is the set of elements that allow several bones to join and articulate together.

For example, the elbow is a joint composed of 3 bones: the humerus, the radius and the ulna.

A joint is generally made up of the following components:
1. Cartilage, which covers the friction surfaces of the bones.
2. Tendons, which attach the muscles to the bones.
3. Ligaments, which hold the joints in place.

At birth, our body has 350 soft bones, which is more than in adulthood because some of them fuse together during our growth until the age of 20-25.

The bone marrow or red marrow occupies all the cavities of the spongy bone, producing 100 to 150 billion red blood cells and 1 to 30 billion white blood cells every day.

The weight of a skeleton is light. It represents about 15% of the body weight.

THE SPINE

The spine supports a large part of the body's weight. It is supported by muscles and ligaments. The spine is the attachment point of the rib cage, pelvis and head. Without the spine, humans would not be able to stand. It also houses the spinal cord.

The spine (also called the rachis), is a stack of jointed bones called vertebrae.

The spine is made up of 24 mobile vertebrae and 9 fused vertebrae:
1. 7 cervical vertebrae
2. 12 dorsal (or thoracic) vertebrae
3. 5 lumbar vertebrae
4. 5 vertebrae forming the sacrum (fused vertebrae)
5. 4 vertebrae forming the coccyx (fused vertebrae)

Between each vertebra is a flexible element, composed of cartilage, and called intervertebral disc. It is thanks to this disc that the spine is mobile.

Each vertebra has a hole (the vertebral cavity). This stack of holes forms the spinal canal, which protects the spinal cord.

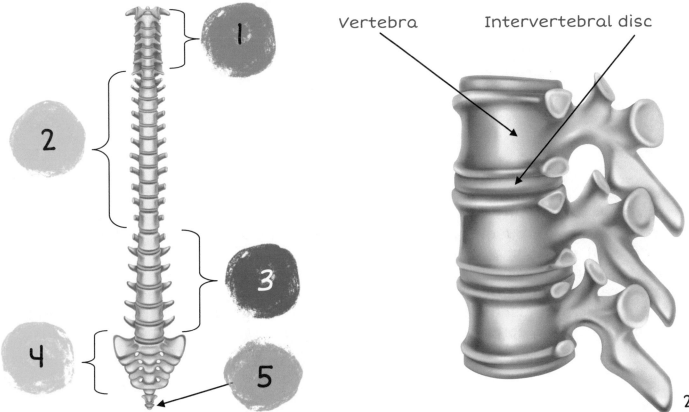

Vertebra   Intervertebral disc

THE SKELETAL MUSCLES

A skeletal muscle is a tissue composed of muscle fibers. Capable of contracting and relaxing, it is used primarily to maintain the body and to carry out movements.

The human body has more than 600 skeletal muscles.
A muscle is composed of muscle fibers, and is attached to the bones by tendons. When these fibers contract, the muscle shortens and causes a movement.

For example, when we bend our arm, our biceps contracts and shortens. When we unfold the arm, it is the opposite: The biceps relaxes, and the triceps contracts in turn.

EXAMPLE: When we bend our arm.

The biceps contracts

The triceps relaxes

Generally, the names of the muscles are related to their location (dorsal muscle, pectoral muscle), their function (hip flexor muscle), or their number of ligament attachments (biceps, triceps).

There are two types of skeletal muscles:
*   Superficial muscles, which are located under the skin and therefore visible during contractions (such as the biceps, pectoralis).
*   The deep muscles, which are located under the superficial muscles.

There are other types of muscles in the body. The striated cardiac muscle (i.e. the heart) and the smooth muscles whose contractions are involuntary (such as the intestine, the uterus, or the blood vessels).

We have 94 muscles in our head, including 43 in our face. When we smile, it is thanks to our muscles. This is the case for each of our facial expressions (and researchers have listed more than 3000 of them!).

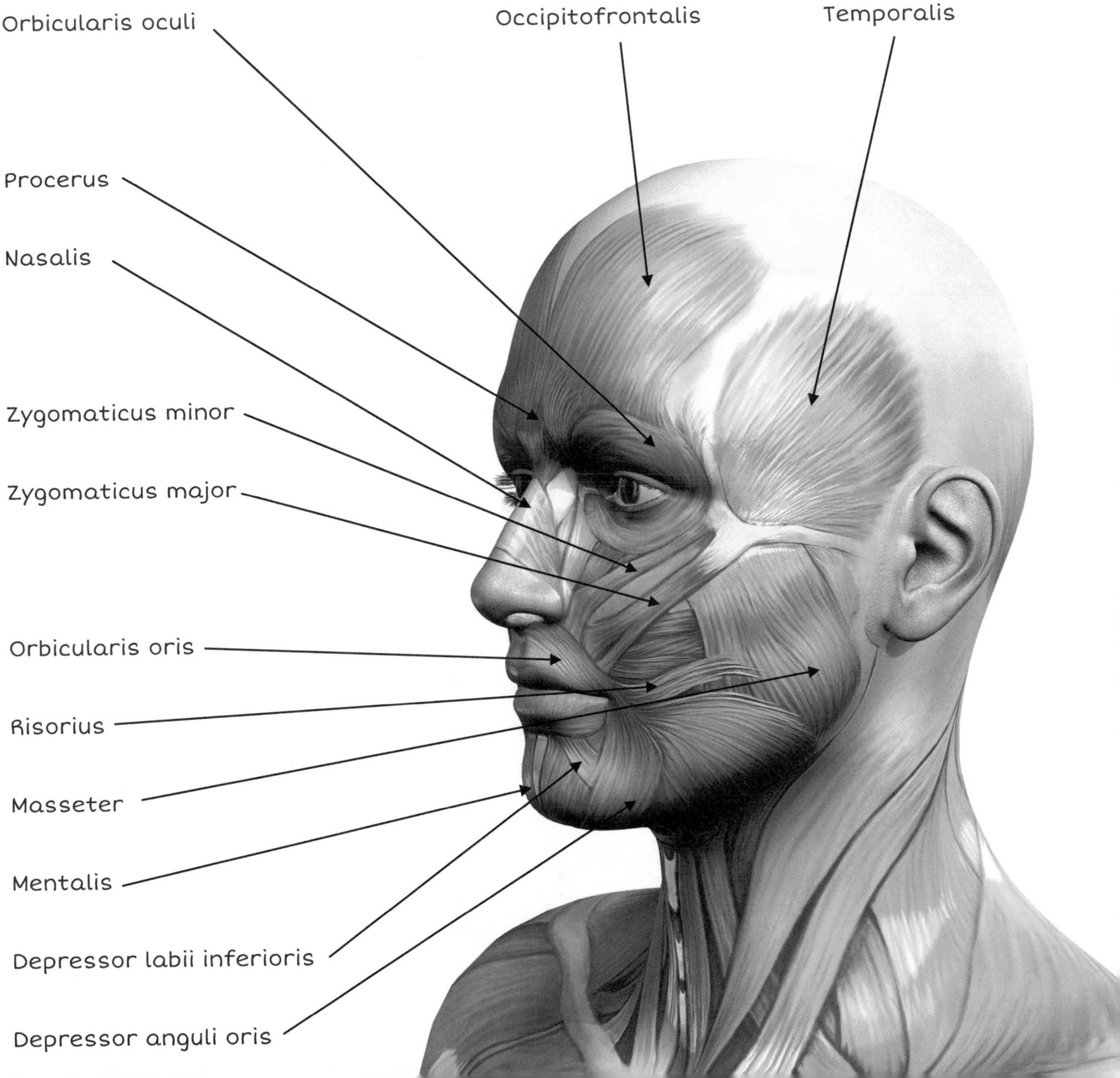

Orbicularis oculi

Occipitofrontalis

Temporalis

Procerus

Nasalis

Zygomaticus minor

Zygomaticus major

Orbicularis oris

Risorius

Masseter

Mentalis

Depressor labii inferioris

Depressor anguli oris

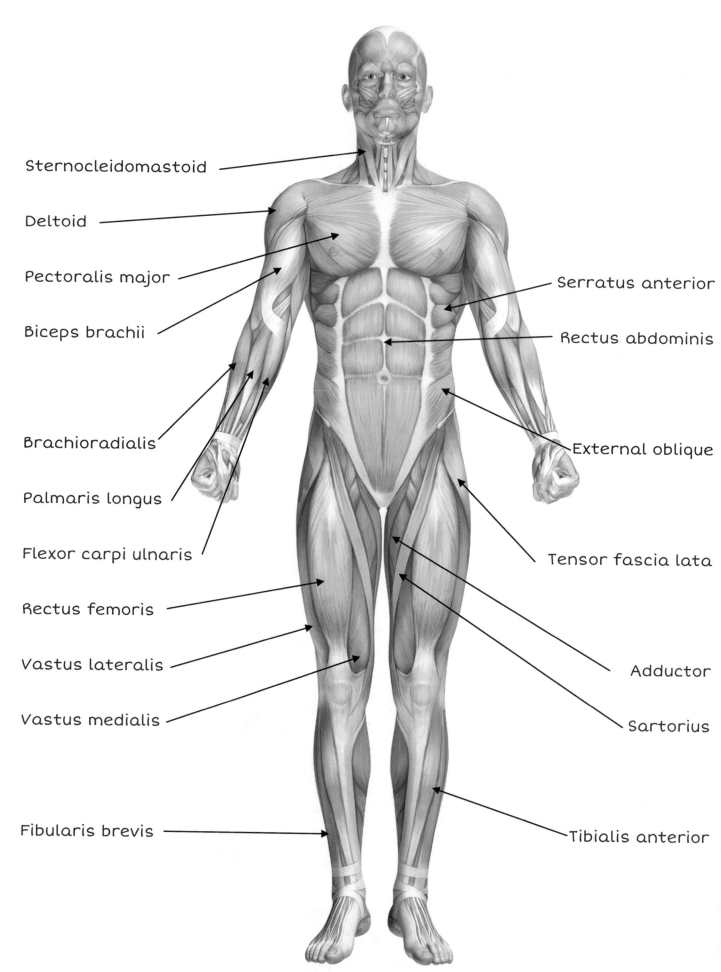

Sternocleidomastoid

Deltoid

Pectoralis major

Biceps brachii

Brachioradialis

Palmaris longus

Flexor carpi ulnaris

Rectus femoris

Vastus lateralis

Vastus medialis

Fibularis brevis

Serratus anterior

Rectus abdominis

External oblique

Tensor fascia lata

Adductor

Sartorius

Tibialis anterior

24

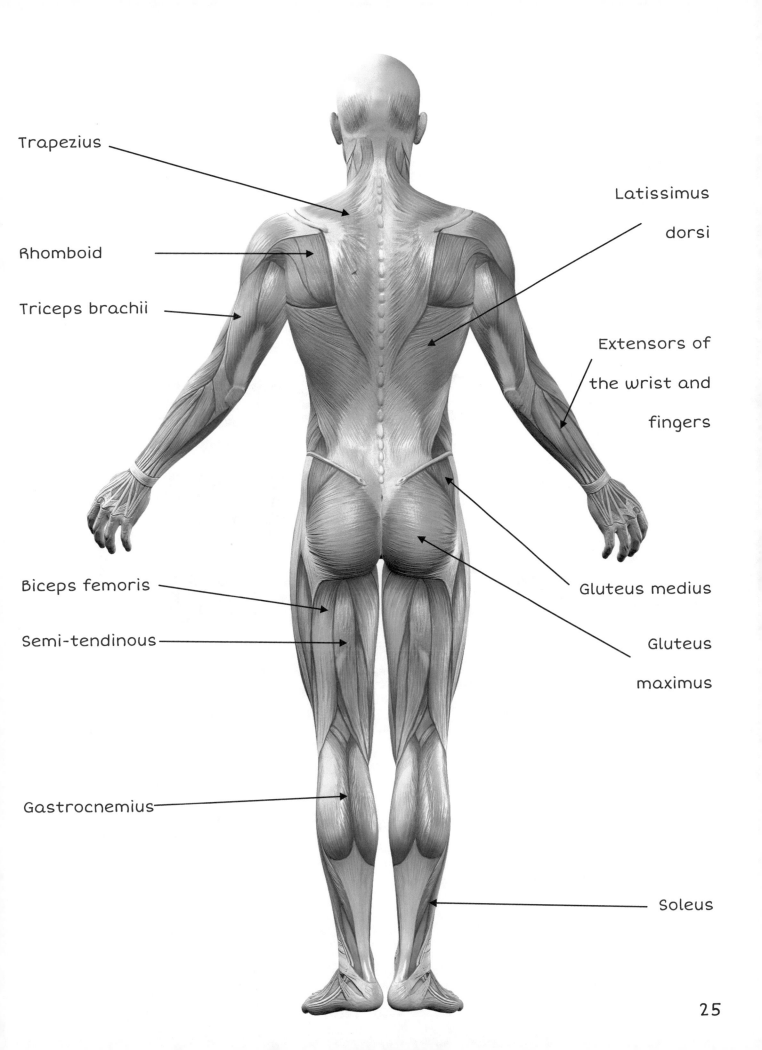

Trapezius

Rhomboid

Triceps brachii

Latissimus dorsi

Extensors of the wrist and fingers

Biceps femoris

Semi-tendinous

Gastrocnemius

Gluteus medius

Gluteus maximus

Soleus

25

THE BRAIN AND THE NERVOUS SYSTEM

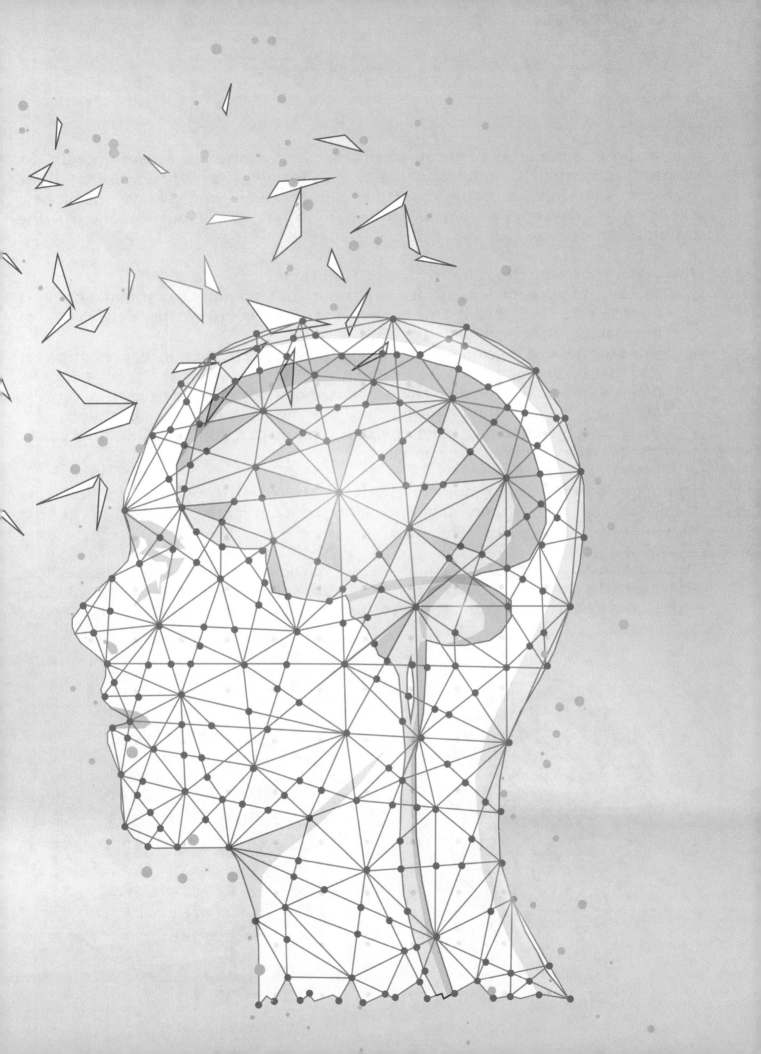

THE BRAIN

The brain is the control center of our body. It manages everything we do, whether consciously or unconsciously. Thanks to its connection with the nervous system, the brain continuously receives and sends messages, creating a permanent communication with our body but also with the outside world.

The brain thus ensures a multitude of functions:

- In an unconscious way (i.e. without us having to think about it ourselves), the brain manages the heartbeat, the secretion of hormones, digestion, growth, etc...
- More or less consciously, it manages emotions, the interpretation of sounds or images, or the coordination of movements. For example, when we walk, we do not think about moving one leg forward after the other. We decide to walk, and it is the brain that manages our walking.
- In a totally conscious way, the brain manages our thinking ability, our imagination, and our decisions.

The brain can manage many functions at the same time. We can walk and think at the same time, while talking to someone and looking at the landscape.

The brain also manages all our reflexes, without us being fully aware of it. For example, if we touch a very hot dish, we immediately withdraw our hand, without thinking about it. It is our brain that manages this reflex movement.

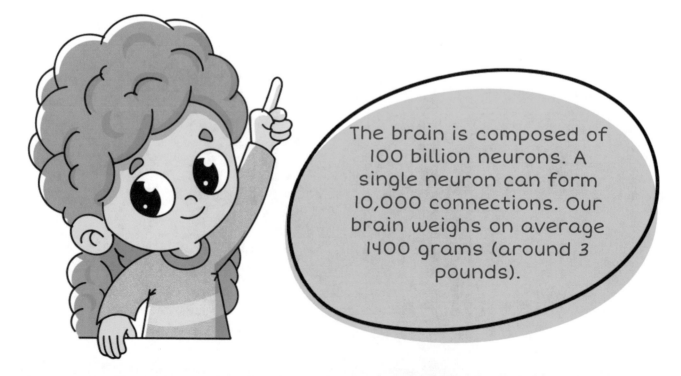

The brain is composed of 100 billion neurons. A single neuron can form 10,000 connections. Our brain weighs on average 1400 grams (around 3 pounds).

The brain is a very complex organ, and is composed of several parts:

- The telencephalon: This is the upper part of the brain, composed of the cortex (which handles sensory functions such as sight or touch, and elaborate functions, such as language and thinking), and the striatum (which handles decision-making). The cortex is divided into different lobes, and each lobe has a defined function.
  The frontal lobe controls thinking, will, and voluntary motor skills.
  The parietal lobe controls perception and the sense of touch.
  The occipital lobe controls visual perception.
  The temporal lobe controls the perception of sounds.
- The diencephalon is located in the middle of the brain and is composed of the thalamus and the hypothalamus. The diencephalon manages the regulation of the nervous system and the hormonal system, but also of sleep.
- The cerebellum is located at the bottom of the brain, towards the back. It manages motor functions, coordination of movements, and balance.
- The brain stem is the lower part of the brain, and is connected to the spinal cord. It is composed of the midbrain and medulla oblongata, which manage basic functions such as attention, involuntary motor functions (such as coughing or sneezing), or cardiac and respiratory movements.

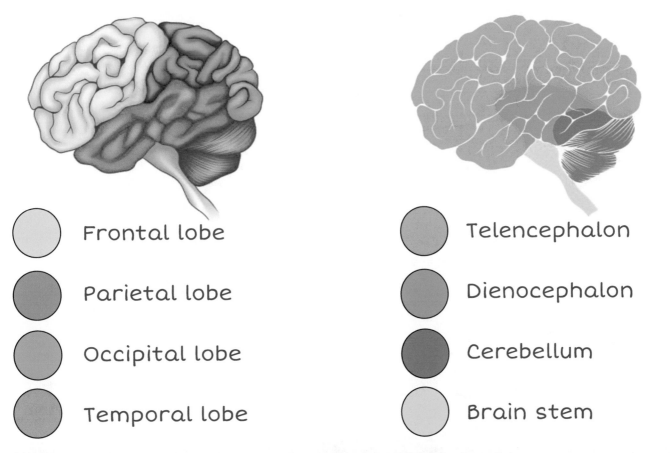

Frontal lobe

Parietal lobe

Occipital lobe

Temporal lobe

Telencephalon

Dienocephalon

Cerebellum

Brain stem

29

THE SPINAL CORD

The spinal cord is a nervous tissue. It is attached to the medulla oblongata, which is attached to the brain. The spinal cord distributes spinal nerves (31 pairs of nerves), between each vertebrae. These nerves allow the transfer of information between the brain and the different organs and limbs of the body.

For example, it is thanks to the spinal cord that we can walk, run, or swim. It is also thanks to the spinal cord that we will feel pain if we step on a sharp stone, because the information goes from the foot through the network of nerves, then reaches the spinal cord, which sends the information to the brain.
Similarly, the spinal cord is how we know when we need to go to the toilet, because the bladder sends the information to the brain.

The spinal cord is very fragile and is almost always impossible to repair. If it is damaged (by an accident or disease), it can have serious consequences, such as paralysis.

The brain and the spinal cord form the central nervous system.

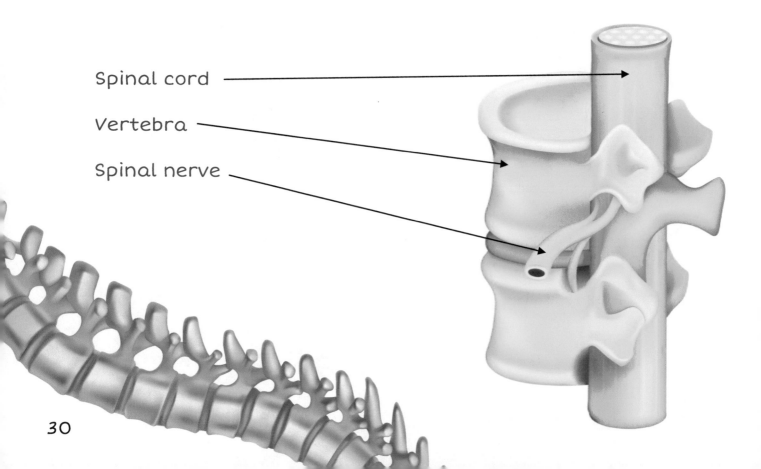

Spinal cord

Vertebra

Spinal nerve

THE NEURONS

A neuron is a nerve communication cell. Neurons are part of both the central nervous system and the peripheral nervous system. We have neurons in the brain, in the spinal cord, and in the nerves.
It is because of neurons that our nervous activity is possible.

A neuron is made up of 3 main components:
1. The cell body, also called the nucleus.
2. The dendrites, which are generally very numerous.
3. The axon (usually only one axon per neuron, but which has many branches).

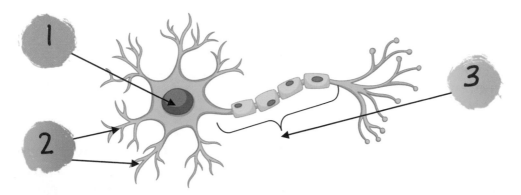

Neurons communicate with each other. When a neuron receives an information, it picks it up with the dendrites, then transmits it immediately to the next neuron thanks to the axon, and so on.
This communication is done by a link called "synapse".

There are two kinds of synapses:
Chemical synapses (The neuron releases a chemical substance called a neurotransmitter, which is picked up by the next neuron), and electrical synapses (The neuron sends an electrical signal to the next neuron).

The speed of communication between neurons is very high. It can reach the speed of 100m/s (330ft/s), that is 360 km/h (224mph).

We don't know exactly how many neurons we have in the body. But scientists estimate that we have 100 billion neurons in the brain, and 500 million in the intestine.

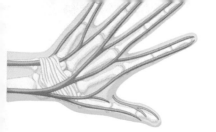

THE NERVES

A nerve is a set of neurons, and more precisely a set of axons, grouped together in a sheath of tissue (cylindrical in shape, like an electric wire).

In simple terms, a nerve is made up of neurons that communicate with each other in a specific area of the body.

For example, the ulnar nerve is a nerve that originates at two cervical and dorsal vertebrae, then travels up the arm, through the elbow and into the last two fingers of the hand. It has a motor function (because it allows the contraction of some muscles of the arm, wrist and hand) and a sensitive function (it participates in the sensitivity of the fingers).

Nerves are organs capable of transmitting information between the brain and the muscles or other organs, in both directions.

Nerves are part of the peripheral nervous system (as opposed to the central nervous system).

There are several types of nerves:
*   Sensory and motor nerves: These are nerves that have a dual function. They transmit information from the organs, muscles and skin to the brain. This is their sensitive function. Their motor function is in a way the opposite of their sensitive function: Once the information has been transmitted to the brain, it is the motor function that manages the reaction. For example, if a person pinches our arm, the nerves will transmit to our brain an information of pain (this is the sensitive function). Our brain will then send an information to our muscles so that we withdraw our arm (this is the motor function).
*   Vegetative nerves: They transmit information from the central nervous system to the different organs or glands, thus ensuring proper physiological functioning (breathing, digestion...)
*   Cranial nerves: There are 12 pairs of cranial nerves. They have a sensory role (like the olfactory, optic, and auditory nerves...), a motor role (like the ocular nerve which controls the movements of our eyes), or a mixed role (i.e. both sensory and motor, like the pneumogastric nerve, also called the vagus nerve, which is used to regulate digestion and the heart rate, but which also ensures the motor functions of the pharynx)
*   The spinal nerves, which are both sensory and motor, and which are attached to the spinal cord.

Nerve impulses, i.e. nerve communication, is an electrical and chemical phenomenon, which is ensured by the neurons.

The nervous system

The longest nerve in the human body is the sciatic nerve. It originates in the spinal cord, crosses the buttocks and the leg and ends in the foot.

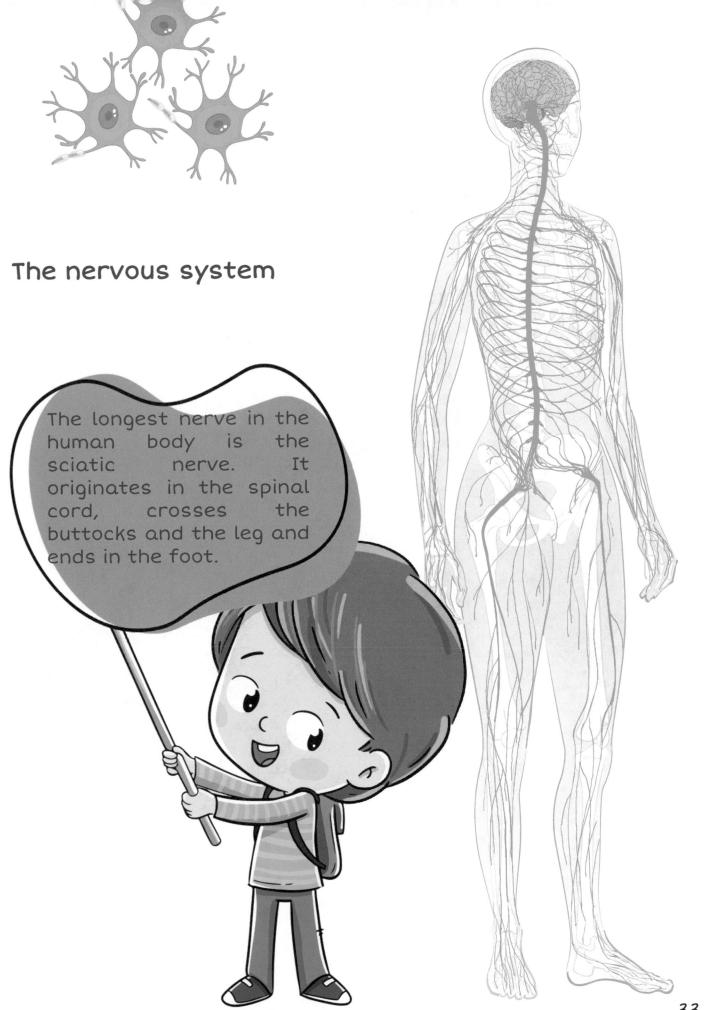

SKIN, HAIR AND BODY HAIR

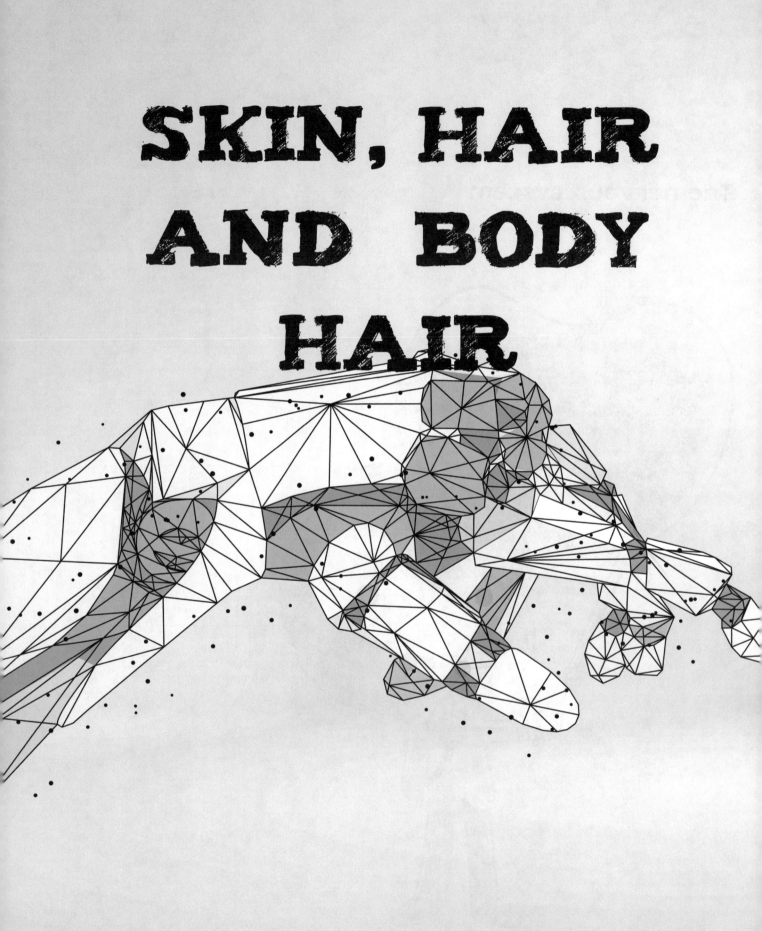

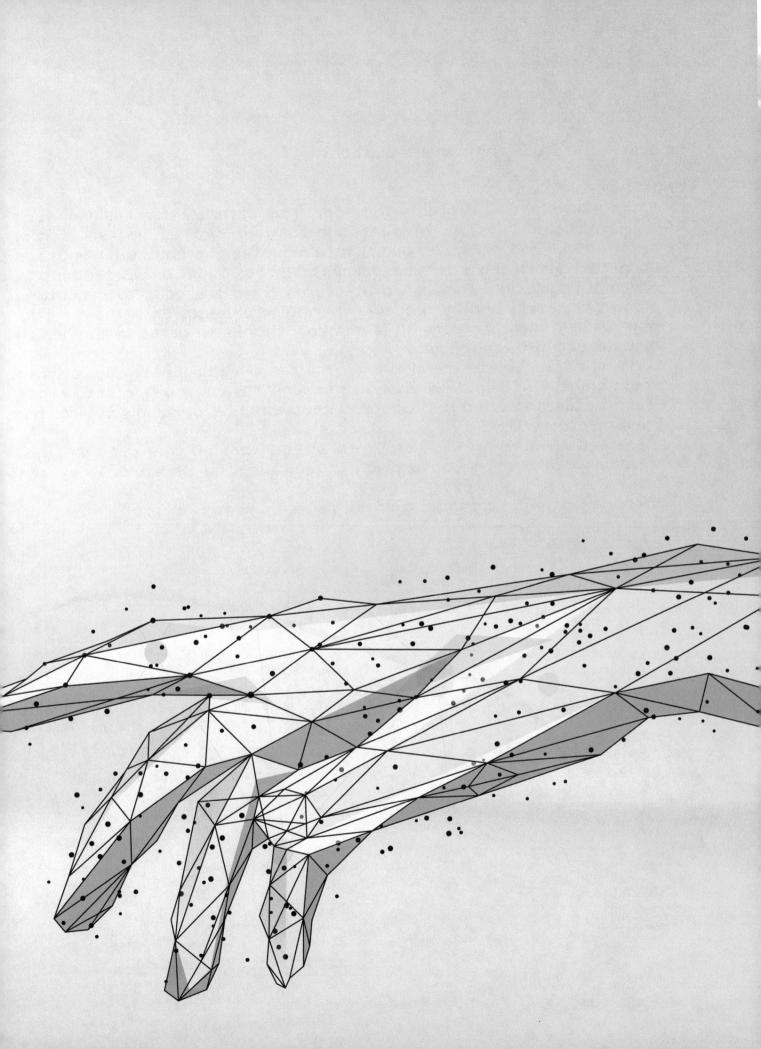

THE SKIN

The skin is the organ that covers our body.

It has several roles:
- Protection: The skin protects the body from external aggressions, such as ultraviolet rays. It prevents certain viruses or bacteria from entering our body. Finally, our skin attenuates the shocks, wounds, or scratches which could damage our muscles, our bones or our tendons.
- Thermal regulation: The skin protects us from the cold, by regulating blood circulation and by reducing thermal exchanges with the outside. But the skin also protects us from heat, thanks to perspiration, which helps the body to cool down.
- Sensitivity and touch: The skin is a very sensitive organ. It allows us to react to heat and cold, to analyze the surfaces we touch, and to sense the pressures exerted and adapt our movements, or simply to feel the wind on our skin.
- Vitamin D production: The skin synthesizes vitamin D thanks to UV rays. Vitamin D allows the absorption of calcium and phosphorus by the intestine.
- Storage: The skin stores a lot of nutrients in its fat cells.

The skin is a fabulous organ: It is able to regenerate quickly (in case of cut for example), but it is especially able to adapt!

When we stay in the sun a lot, our skin tans. This is how it protects itself from UV rays. The skin can also thicken according to our habits, our lifestyles, our occupations: If a person plays the guitar regularly, the skin on his fingertips will become thicker. If a person does manual work, the skin on their hands will thicken. And if someone regularly puts on shoes that cause friction, then the skin on their ankles or feet will also thicken.

The skin is the largest and heaviest organ in the human body. The skin of an adult has a total surface area of about 2m² (21.5 ft²) and weighs about 5kg (11 lbs).

The skin is composed of 3 layers:

1. The epidermis: This is the top layer of the skin. In reality, the epidermis is made up of 5 different layers. The upper layer of the epidermis is mainly made up of dead cells. It is the epidermis that protects us from viruses for example.

2. The dermis: The dermis is located under the epidermis. It is a thick and elastic layer, which protects us especially from shocks. The dermis contains many blood vessels, sebaceous glands (which produce sebum, allowing to hydrate the skin and participating in the protection against microbes), and the roots of hair and hairs. It is also the dermis that contains the sensory cells so important for our sense of touch.

3. The hypodermis: The hypodermis is the deepest layer of the skin. It also contains blood vessels, but also adipose cells (i.e. fat cells). The hypodermis is in contact with the muscles or bones (4).

We do not all have the same skin color, and this depends on our origins.

Skin color is determined by a substance called melanin. The more melanin the skin contains, the darker it is. And the darker the skin, the more it blocks the sun's rays.

Our ancestors, originally from Africa, had dark skin (there is a lot of sun in Africa!). Then, some populations migrated to Europe. Over the generations, their skin adapted and became lighter, because there is less sun in Europe. Some populations migrated to Asia, and there again the skin has adapted.

This is why there are many different skin colors.

HAIR AND BODY HAIR

Hair and body hair have a similar function.

The hair protects the head, and thus essentially the brain. Hair can protect from cold or heat, or from the sun.

Body hair has different roles depending on its location: It can protect against friction and irritation for example. They protect against the cold. They also serve to retain odors, including pheromones, which are substances that play an important role in sexual attraction.

Nose hairs filter the air we breathe, thus preventing dust or microbes from entering our body.

The hairs are also real antennas: they allow us to pick up a vibration, or a displacement of air.

The average adult has 120,000 hairs on his or her head. Each hair has a lifespan of 6 years, and we lose between 50 and 100 hairs per day.

A healthy hair can support a very important weight, up to 2 kg (4.4 lbs)

Hair is composed of keratin, and has several elements:

1. The hair shaft: This is the visible part of the hair, whose color varies according to individuals. The shaft is composed of three layers: The medulla, which is the central part and is composed of a fatty substance. The cortex, which is the main component of the hair and is composed of keratin, proteins and lipids. The cuticle, which is the outer layer of the hair, composed mainly of keratin and whose surface is covered with small scales, arranged like the tiles of a house.

2. The root: Located under the skin, it is the living part of the hair. The root is mainly composed of a bulb, which is itself connected to small blood vessels.

3. The sebaceous gland: It is not really part of the hair, but it is essential. Located just above the bulb, it allows the lubrication of the hair.

4. The arrector muscle: This tiny muscle, attached to the bulb, is responsible for the erection phenomenon. It is thanks to this muscle that our hairs sometimes stand up when we are cold or afraid.

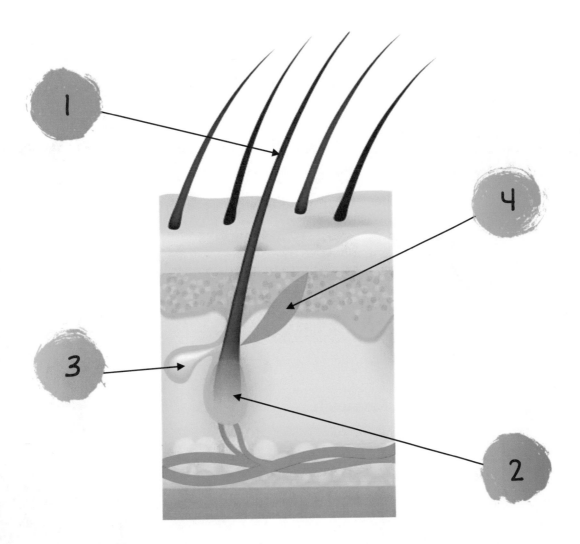

BLOOD CIRCULATION AND RESPIRATORY SYSTEM

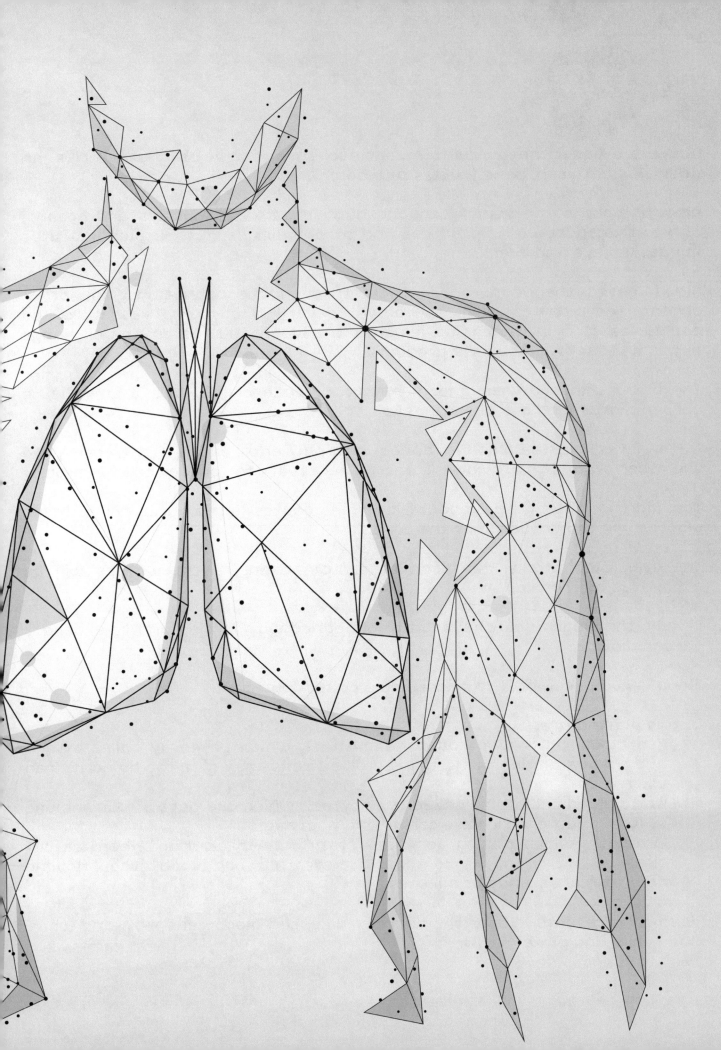

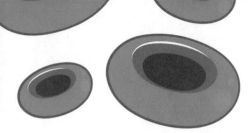

BLOOD

Blood is a liquid that circulates continuously in our veins and arteries. An adult has between 4 and 6 liters of blood.

Blood is used to deliver oxygen and nutrients to our muscles and organs, and to transport waste products and carbon dioxide to their disposal sites (lungs, kidneys and liver).

Blood leaves the heart and travels through the arteries to the other organs. The arteries carry the blood to very small blood vessels called capillaries. It is in the capillaries that the blood and the organs exchange nutrients, gases, and waste products.

The blood brings oxygen and nutrients to each organ, and then collects carbon dioxide and metabolic waste.

In the intestine, the blood is loaded with nutrients, which it then brings to the other organs to provide the energy necessary for proper cell function.

The kidneys filter the blood of certain wastes (urea, uric acid). These wastes will be evacuated by the urine.

The liver also filters the blood of certain toxins. These wastes will be evacuated by the bile.

Finally, the lungs allow the blood to be loaded with oxygen and to evacuate carbon dioxide.

Blood is composed of a colorless liquid called "plasma".

In this plasma are:
- Red blood cells (also called haematids), which primarily carry oxygen and carbon dioxide. It is the red blood cells that give the blood its red color.
- White blood cells (also called leukocytes), which are part of our immune system and fight viruses, germs and bacteria.
- Platelets, which play a very important role in clotting. When we cut ourselves, it is thanks to the platelets that our blood stops flowing after a few seconds or minutes.

Plasma represents 55% of the blood volume, red blood cells 44%, and white blood cells and platelets 1%.

VEINS AND ARTERIES

Arteries are the blood vessels that carry blood to the organs. At the exit of the heart, the main artery, called the aorta, is the largest artery in the human body. It divides into two other arteries (the iliac arteries), which in turn divide again and again to supply the capillaries. The arteries therefore carry the blood loaded with oxygen and nutrients.

Arteries are shown in red in the drawing below.

Veins are the blood vessels that carry blood from the organs back to the heart. Veins carry blood that is loaded with carbon dioxide.

Veins are shown in blue in the drawing below.

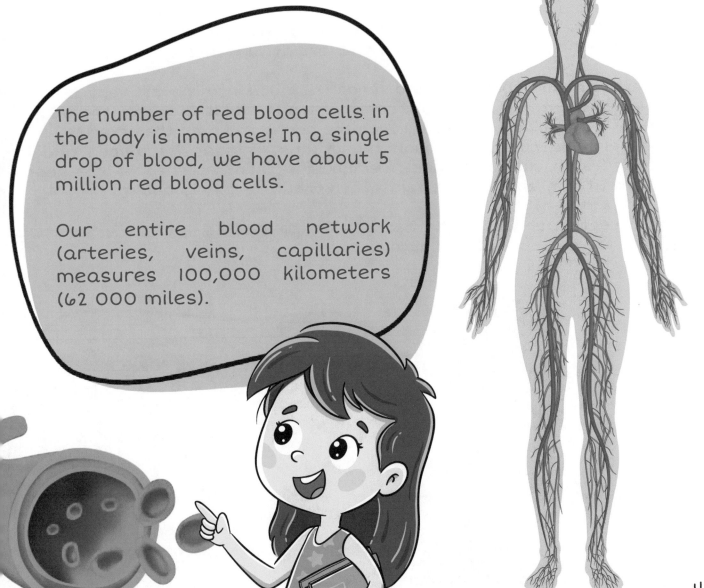

The number of red blood cells in the body is immense! In a single drop of blood, we have about 5 million red blood cells.

Our entire blood network (arteries, veins, capillaries) measures 100,000 kilometers (62 000 miles).

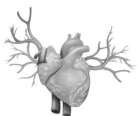

THE HEART

The heart is located in the rib cage. It acts as a pump that sends blood throughout the body.

The heart is a hollow muscle, divided into two parts (the left heart and the right heart). The wall separating these two parts is called the septum.
Each part is divided into two: the ventricle and the atrium. These two parts are separated by membranes called valves.

Here is how the heart works:
1. The right atrium fills with blood from the organs. This blood comes in through the upper and lower vena cava and contains carbon dioxide. When the right atrium is full, it contracts and sends blood into the right ventricle.
2. When the right ventricle is full, it contracts and sends blood to the lungs through the pulmonary artery.
3. In the lungs, the blood gets rid of carbon dioxide and is enriched with oxygen. Then the blood goes to the left atrium through the pulmonary veins.
4. The left atrium contracts and sends the blood into the left ventricle.
5. The left ventricle, once full, contracts and sends blood to the body's organs. This blood passes through the aorta and then the arteries.
6. The blood circulates through the organs, unloads its oxygen and is loaded with carbon dioxide. The blood is then returned to the heart (right atrium) through the veins. Then the cycle starts again.

The contraction phase of the heart is called systole, and the relaxation phase of the heart is called diastole.

At rest, your heart beats about 70 times a minute, which represents about 6 liters of blood expelled.
But the heart of a very athletic adult can pump up to 35 liters of blood per minute during exercise.

If you want to know how big your heart is, just clench your fist! This is approximately the size of your heart.

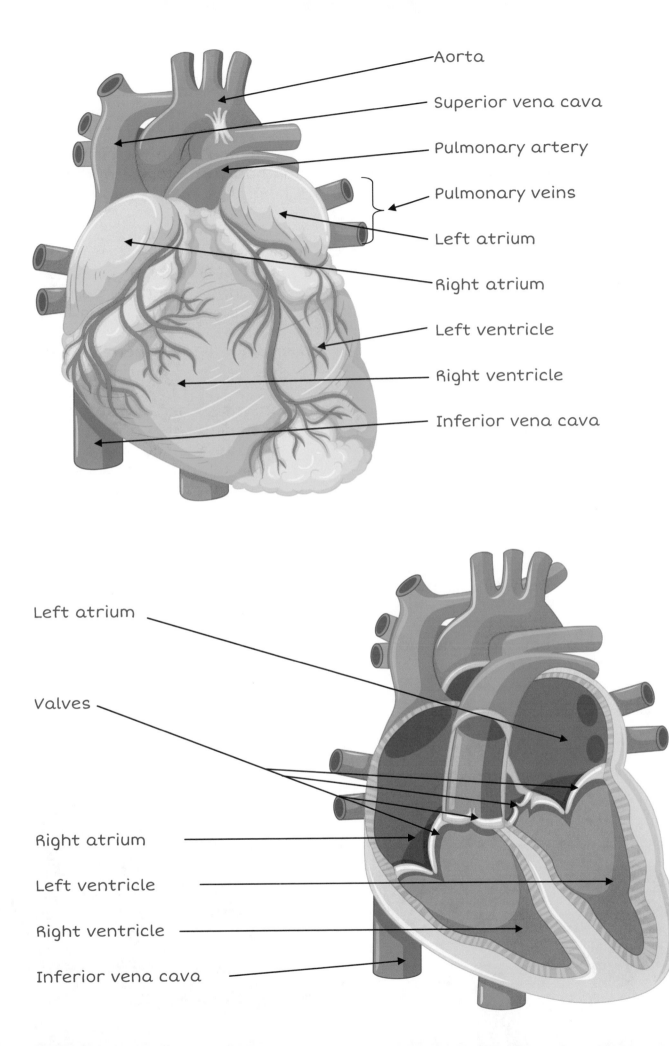

Aorta

Superior vena cava

Pulmonary artery

Pulmonary veins

Left atrium

Right atrium

Left ventricle

Right ventricle

Inferior vena cava

Left atrium

Valves

Right atrium

Left ventricle

Right ventricle

Inferior vena cava

45

THE LUNGS

The lungs are the organs of respiration. They are located in the rib cage. The human being has two lungs: The right lung has three lobes, and the left lung has two lobes. They are enveloped in a kind of very thin bag called the pleura.

During inspiration, the diaphragm and the intercostal muscles contract. The rib cage increases in volume and its internal pressure decreases (which causes a call of outside air). Thus, air enters the lungs. When we exhale, the diaphragm relaxes, the rib cage lowers, and the lungs deflate. Thus, the air leaves our body, through the mouth or nose.
When we breathe in, it is oxygen that enters our body. When we exhale, carbon dioxide leaves our body.

The air enters our body through our mouth or nose, then passes through the pharynx (behind the nose and the mouth) and larynx (in our neck). It then reaches the trachea and the bronchi. The bronchial tubes are like two pipes, which lead the air to our two lungs. In the lungs, the bronchi divide into smaller structures until they become bronchioles. It's a bit like a tree: there is the trunk (the bronchus), then the roots, which are smaller and smaller (the bronchioles).
The bronchioles allow the air to arrive in the pulmonary alveoli, which are very small bags with very thin walls. The alveoli are very vascularized, that is to say that many tiny veins surround them. These veins are called blood capillaries.

It is in the alveoli that the blood is discharged of carbon dioxide and is loaded with oxygen.

All of our lung alveoli have a surface area the size of a volleyball court.

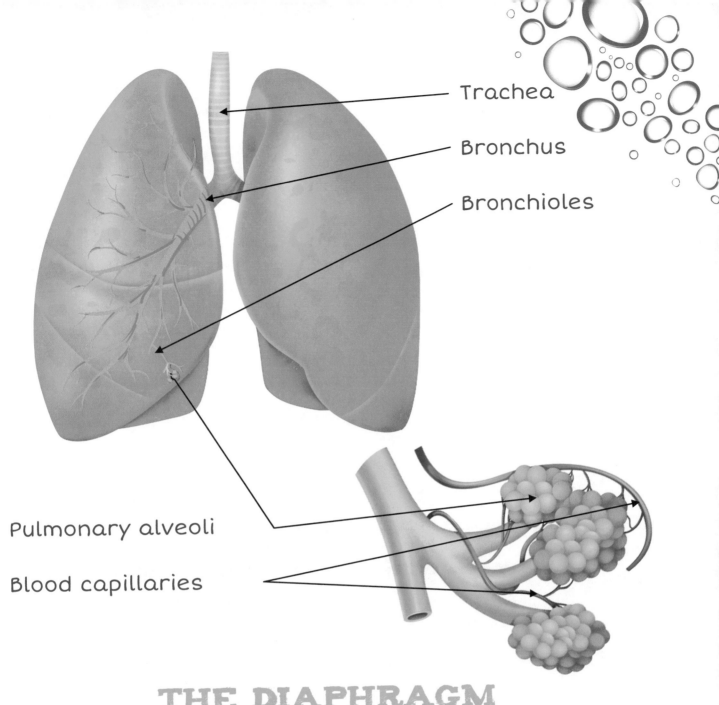

Trachea

Bronchus

Bronchioles

Pulmonary alveoli

Blood capillaries

THE DIAPHRAGM

The diaphragm is a muscular membrane that separates the rib cage from the abdominal cavity.

It is involved in breathing (we breathe thanks to its contractions), but also in digestion (its contractions help our food go to the stomach).

When we sneeze, it is because our diaphragm contracts to expel a foreign body (a dust for example). When we cough, it is also because of our diaphragm, which contracts to expel a foreign body or mucus that is blocking our airways.

THE HEAD

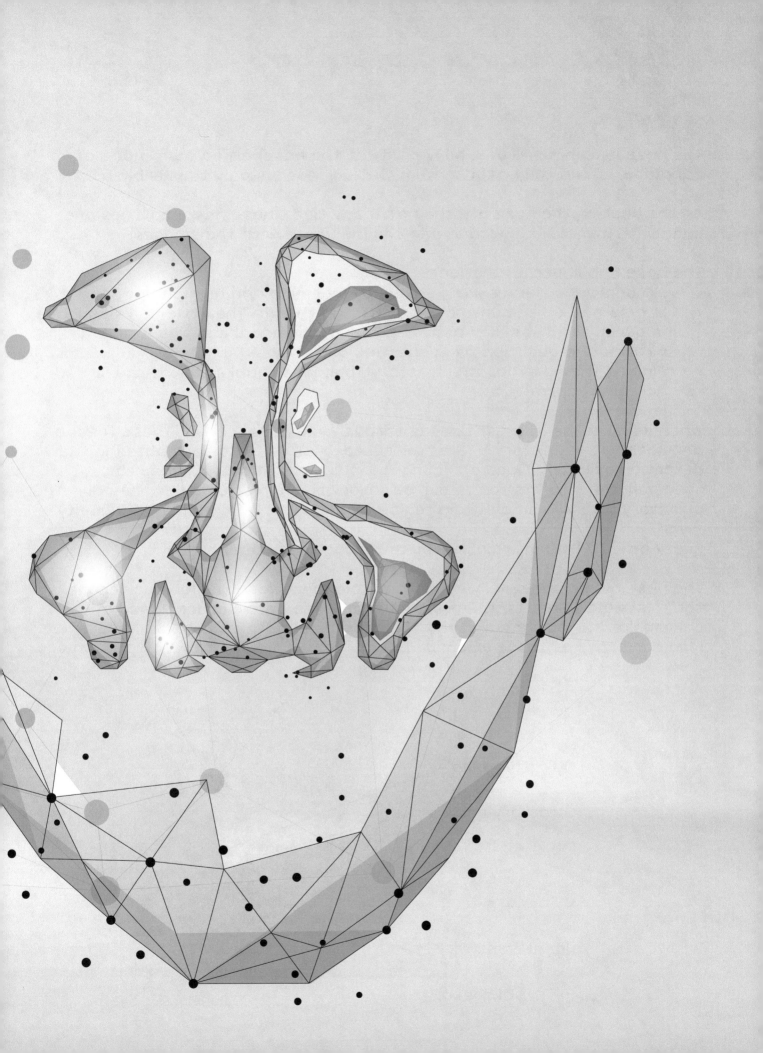

THE NOSE

The nose is composed of a bony part (at the base) and a part made of cartilage, called the nasal septum. But our nose is only the visible part.

At the back of the nose are the nasal cavities. These nasal cavities are lined with mucous membrane and communicate with the sinuses.

The nose has several functions:
- It conditions the air we breathe, by warming and humidifying it.
- It also has an immune role, by filtering the air. The little hairs we have in our nostrils, as well as the mucus in our nasal cavities, prevent viruses and pollution from entering our body.
- Finally, the nose has an olfactory role. It is thanks to it that we perceive odors.

When we breathe in air, it passes through the nasal cavity. These fossae are lined with olfactory nerves (or receptors), i.e. cells specialized in the detection of odors. Once an odorant molecule is captured, the cells transmit the information to our olfactory bulb which decodes the odor. The olfactory bulb is a small brain region located just above the nasal cavity.

Every day, 20,000 liters of air pass through our nose.

The nose also plays a very important role in taste. Although the tongue is the first to distinguish flavors, many airborne particles (released by chewing) enter our nasal cavity through the pharynx. This explains why we lose our sense of taste when we have a cold.

Olfactory bulb

Olfactory nerves

Nasal cavity

(or nasal fossa)

THE SINUSES

The sinuses are a set of symmetrical cavities located on each side of the nose and forehead (above the eyes).

There are different types of sinuses:

- The maxillary sinuses (the largest) located in the cheekbones.
- The frontal sinuses, located in the center of the lower part of the forehead.
- The ethmoid sinuses, located between the eyes at the base of the nose.
- The sphenoid sinuses, located behind the nasal cavity.

The sinuses are lined with a mucous membrane, itself covered with a thin layer of mucus. Normally these cavities are filled with air, but when we are sick, they can fill with mucus.

The sinuses help to warm the air we breathe in, and also participate in the resonance of our voice. Finally, they reduce the weight of the skull, since they are hollow.

Frontal sinuses

Sphenoid sinuses

Ethmoid Sinuses

Maxillary Sinuses

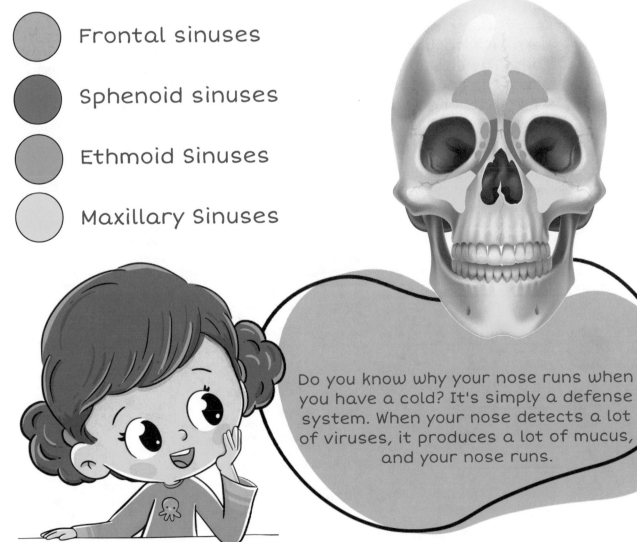

Do you know why your nose runs when you have a cold? It's simply a defense system. When your nose detects a lot of viruses, it produces a lot of mucus, and your nose runs.

THE EYES

The eye is the organ of sight. It is a complex organ, both in its anatomy and in its functioning.

The eye, also called eyeball, is composed of several elements:

1. The sclera has the function of protecting the eye, and is surrounded by a membrane called conjunctiva. It is the white part of the eye.
2. The cornea is located on the front of the eye. It is transparent. Its role is to transmit the light to the lens and the retina.
3. The iris is the colored part of the eye. It is a disc-shaped membrane, perforated in its center by the pupil. The iris contracts or dilates according to the luminosity.
4. The pupil is a hole in the center of the iris. Depending on the contraction or dilation of the iris, the pupil enlarges or shrinks, thus regulating the light intensity in the eye.
5. The crystalline lens is the lens of the eye. It is located behind the iris. It also allows light to pass to the retina, but also allows the phenomenon of accommodation, that is to say that it allows to adjust the vision (a bit like the lens of a camera, or the adjustment wheel on binoculars).
6. The retina is a thin membrane that covers the inner surface of the eye. It is very sensitive to light. It is composed of photoreceptors called cones and rods. The cones allow us to see colors, as well as the details of what we see. The rods allow us to see when there is little light.
7. The optic nerve, attached to the back of the eye, sends information to the brain.
8. The vitreous humor (or vitreous body) is a thick, clear liquid that fills the inside of our eye.

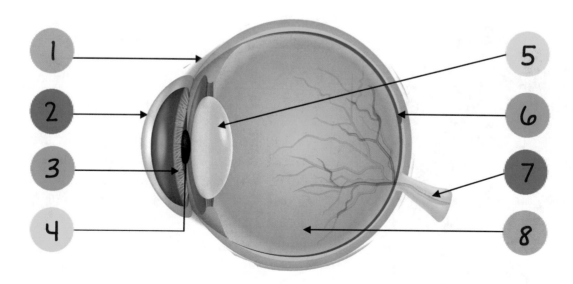

To understand how vision works, we have to understand that in reality we do not see objects (or landscapes, or people). In reality, we see the light that is reflected on these objects. This is why when we are in total darkness, we see nothing.

This is how vision works:
- Light reflects off an object we are looking at.
- This light enters the eye through the cornea. It is regulated by the iris and the pupil, then reaches our lens.
- The lens adapts to make the image sharp, depending on the distance to the object. But since the lens is small and "bulging", the image of the object is reversed! Concretely, our eye sees the object upside down.
- The light then passes into the vitreous humor and reaches the retina.
- The retina transforms the information it receives into electrical impulses, which are then sent to the brain by the optic nerve.
- The brain interprets the signals it receives and puts the perceived image back in the right direction.

And since we have two eyes, we perceive two different images. Thus, the brain can interpret the relief, depth and distance of objects.

The human eye can distinguish 10 million different shades of color.

Our eyes move thanks to 6 small muscles called oculomotor muscles. We can't see them because they are attached to the back of the eye.

THE EARS

Our two ears are the organs of hearing.

An ear is composed of three parts:

- The external ear: This is the visible part of our ear. It consists of the pinna (1) (the outer part of the ear, made of cartilage), the ear canal (2) (the hole in our ear), and the eardrum or tympanic membrane (3) (which is a membrane at the bottom of the ear canal, and which we cannot see).
- The middle ear: It is the continuity of the ear canal. It is composed of three small bones called ossicles (the smallest bones of the human body). The malleus (4), the incus (5), and the stapes (6). These three bones are connected to the eardrum on one side, and to the inner ear on the other side. There is also a small organ called the Eustachian tube (7), which connects the middle ear to the nasopharynx. The eustachian tube acts as a valve to regulate the air pressure on either side of the eardrum.
- The inner ear: It is located beyond the middle ear. It is composed of the cochlea (8) (also called the snail), the semicircular canals (9), the vestibule (10) and the auditory nerves (11). The inner ear is filled with fluid.

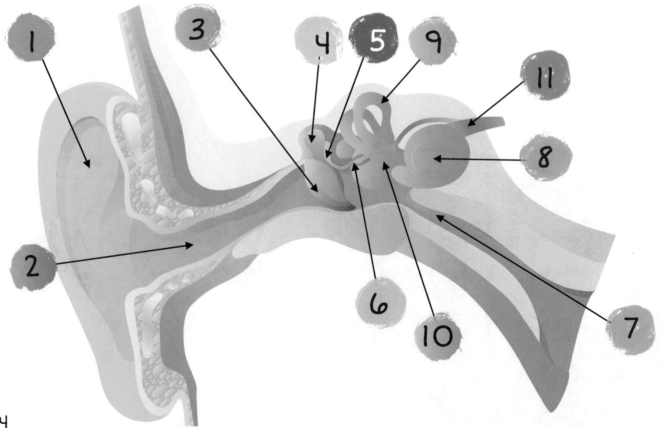

To understand how our ear works, we must first understand how sound works.

A sound is a vibration that moves through the air at a speed of 340 meters per second (760 mph).

Here is what happens in our ear:

- The sound is picked up by the pinna and then travels into the ear canal.
- The vibration of the sound causes the eardrum to vibrate.
- As the eardrum vibrates, it activates the ossicles (malleus, incus, stapes), which in turn transmit this vibration to the cochlea.
- In the cochlea there are microscopic hairs. The vibration propagates through the fluid in the cochlea, and the small hairs (or cilia) also begin to vibrate.
- The cilia convert the sound vibration into an electrical signal, which is then transmitted to the brain by the auditory nerves.
- The brain then interprets the signal. It is at this precise moment that we identify what we hear.

The ear is the organ of hearing... But it also plays a very important role in our sense of balance! It is the role of the semicircular canals: They allow the brain to detect the changes of position of the head.

THE MOUTH

The mouth is the common name for the oral cavity. This oral cavity is closed by the lips, and ends at the pharynx.

The oral cavity has different roles, including chewing and swallowing (which are the first processes of digestion), identification of flavors, and speech (by allowing us to modulate sounds and also by serving as a sounding board for our voice).
It also plays a role in breathing (the air we breathe can enter or leave our body through the mouth or nose).

The oral cavity is composed of several organs, including the tongue and teeth. It also contains salivary glands (under the tongue and in the lower jaw).

Our mouth contains more bacteria than people on earth!

In fact, even with very good oral hygiene, our mouth is populated with about 10 billion bacteria.

THE SALIVARY GLANDS

The salivary glands ensure the secretion of saliva. Saliva is always present in our mouth.
It is mainly composed of water, but also of proteins and minerals.
It is mainly used to moisten food to facilitate chewing and contains enzymes (i.e. proteins) that break down food to make it easier to digest.
Saliva also protects our mouth by moistening and lubricating it (it is very unpleasant to have a dry mouth) and by protecting us from certain microbes. Finally, saliva regulates the acidity of our mouth, helps to heal small wounds, and contributes to the protection of the dental enamel.

Most of our saliva is produced by three pairs of salivary glands:
1. The parotid glands, located in the corner of the lower jaw.
2. The sublingual glands, located under the tongue.
3. The submandibular glands, located under the lower jaw.

There are many other tiny salivary glands located throughout the oral cavity.

Our mouth can produce up to 1.5 liters of saliva per day.

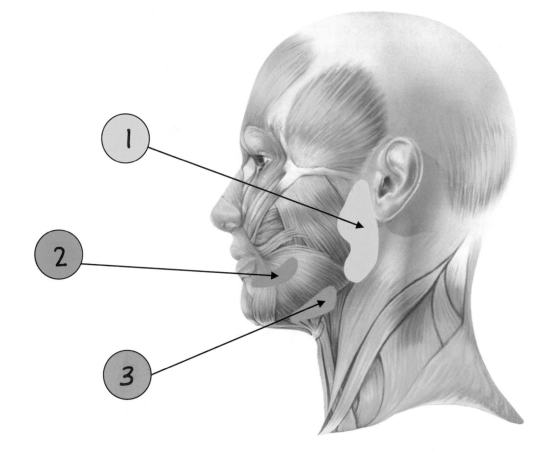

THE TONGUE

The tongue originates from the hyoid bone (just above the larynx) and is composed of 17 muscles. The surface of the tongue is covered with a mucous membrane containing 10,000 sensors (taste buds). It is a very mobile organ. Under our tongue is a cord (called the frenulum), which prevents the tongue from tilting backwards (which could cause choking).

The tongue has several functions:
- Chewing: The tongue helps with chewing (the act of chewing food) by moving food around in the mouth.
- Swallowing: By synchronizing with the larynx, the tongue allows us to swallow our food towards the esophagus.
- Phonation: The tongue (but also the lips, the teeth and the lower jaw) allows us to modulate the sounds we produce when we speak. Without the tongue, we would not be able to pronounce certain sounds and letters, and therefore most of the words in our language.
- Taste identification: The tongue is the organ that allows us to perceive the taste of our food (or anything else we put in our mouth).

Here is how taste perception works:
- The surface of our tongue is lined with taste buds that are able to detect flavors through their receptor cells.
- The taste buds do not all have the same function. Some detect sweet flavors, others salty flavors, others bitter flavors...
- Once the flavor is detected, the cells transmit a chemical message to the brain, thanks to neurotransmitters.
- This message goes to different regions of the brain (including the thalamus, the hypothalamus and the cortex). Thus, the brain analyzes the flavor but also the sensations. This explains why we can like or dislike certain flavors, and why certain foods can create emotions, or recall memories.

Let's also note that the tongue, but also the whole oral cavity, allows us to detect sensations related to tasting. We can thus detect if a food is crunchy or soft, if it is dry or creamy, if it is hard or liquid...

THE TEETH

Teeth are essential to the chewing process. They serve to grind our food, allowing a better swallowing, and facilitating digestion. Finally, our teeth have a role in diction. Without them, it would be difficult to pronounce certain sounds.

A tooth is an organ crossed by small nerve bundles and irrigated by small blood vessels.

A tooth is composed of 3 parts:
- The crown: This is the visible part of the tooth, made up of enamel (1) (the outer white part), dentin (2) (mineral material also called ivory), and pulp (3) (tissue containing the nerves and blood vessels).
- The collar or the neck (4): This is the junction point between the crown and the root.
- The root (5): This is the non-visible part of the tooth, which is attached to the jawbone, itself covered by the gum. The root consists of dentin and a pulp canal (extension of the pulp into each root of the tooth).

A child has 20 teeth, which are called baby teeth. These are temporary teeth that grow in from the age of 6 months. From the age of 6 years, the milk teeth start to fall out and are replaced by the permanent teeth.
An adult has 32 teeth.

We have different types of teeth:
- Incisors: These are the front teeth. They are used to cut food.
- Canines: They are located on each side of the incisors and are used to tear food.
- Premolars and molars: Located towards the back of the mouth, they are used to crush food.
- Wisdom teeth: These are molars that grow in late adolescence or adulthood.

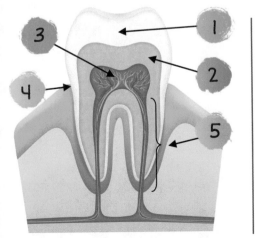

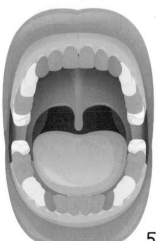

In adulthood, we have :
- 8 incisors (in red)
- 4 canines (in blue)
- 8 premolars (yellow)
- 8 molars (green)
- 4 wisdom teeth (in white)

THE NECK AND THE THROAT

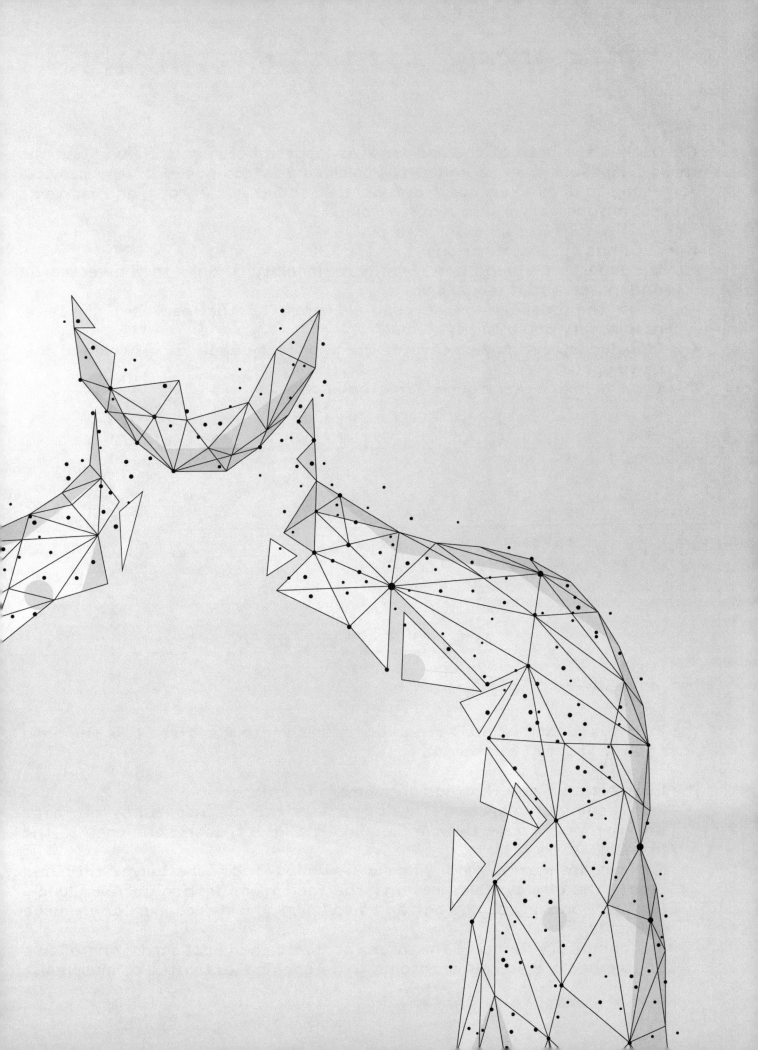

THE NECK AND THE THROAT

The neck is the area of the body that is located between the head and the thorax. Its back part is called the neck and is composed of the cervical vertebrae and muscles. Its front part is called the throat and contains several organs (larynx, pharynx, thyroid).

The neck has several functions:
- It supports the head and gives it its mobility (thanks to the vertebrae and muscles that make it up).
- It is the passage of several elements of the nervous, digestive, respiratory and blood systems.
- It includes several elements of the phonatory apparatus (which allows us to speak)
- It plays a role in the general metabolism.

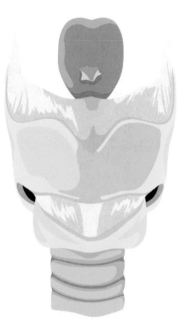

THE LARYNX

The larynx is a cartilaginous organ of the respiratory system. It is the hard part on the front of our throat.

The larynx is an organ that has three main functions:
- The respiratory function: The larynx lets the air inspired by the nose and the mouth pass through, leading it to the trachea and then to the bronchi.
- The swallowing function: When we swallow food, the larynx tilts and blocks the airway. This prevents the food from getting into our lungs. Put one hand on your throat and swallow. You will feel your larynx move upwards.
- The phonatory function: The larynx protects the vocal cords, and allows us to modulate sounds according to its opening (activated by muscles).

THE VOCAL CORDS

The vocal cords are muscular organs, located in the larynx. These two membranes, which are white or very pale pink in color, can contract or relax.

When we breathe, they relax. When we swallow food, they contract.

It is thanks to our vocal cords that we can speak, sing, or even shout. Under the effect of the larynx, the passage of air makes our vocal cords vibrate, and we can thus produce sounds (which we articulate later with our mouth, lips, and tongue).

The action of speaking is called phonation.

THE THYROID

The thyroid is a small gland located in the neck, below the Adam's apple. It is shaped like a butterfly.

The thyroid secretes thyroid hormones that control the rate of chemical functions in the body.

These hormones stimulate the body's tissues to produce proteins, and can increase the amount of oxygen used by the cells.

Thyroid hormones affect many vital body functions, such as heart rate, energy expenditure, growth, heat production, fertility and digestion.

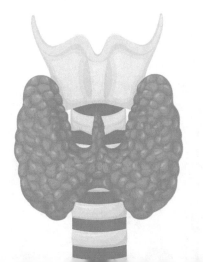

THE PHARYNX

The pharynx is a hollow muscular tube. It originates behind the nose, passes to the back of the oral cavity, and then descends along the neck to the back of the larynx and joins the esophagus.

Like the larynx, the pharynx has several roles:
- The respiratory function: The pharynx allows air to pass from the nasal cavity to the larynx.
- The swallowing function: Through the action of different muscles, the pharynx ensures the transit of food or liquids from the mouth to the esophagus. The larynx prevents food from going to the lungs, and the uvula (which is part of the pharynx and is the little piece of flesh that hangs at the back of your mouth) prevents food from going to the nasal cavity.
- The phonatory function: When the vocal cords vibrate in the larynx, the pharynx plays a role of amplification and resonance of sounds.

The pharynx is also connected to the Eustachian tubes, which are part of the auditory system.

Finally, the pharynx houses the tonsils. The tonsils, located at the back of our throat, have the ability to filter microorganisms such as bacteria and viruses. The immune cells in the tonsils produce antibodies that help destroy these microbes.

The pharynx is composed of three parts:
- The nasopharynx, the upper part that communicates with the nasal cavity.
- The oropharynx is connected to the oral cavity and contains the uvula and tonsils.
- The hypopharynx, the lower part that communicates with the esophagus.

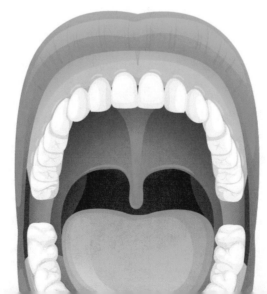

NECK AND THROAT ANATOMY

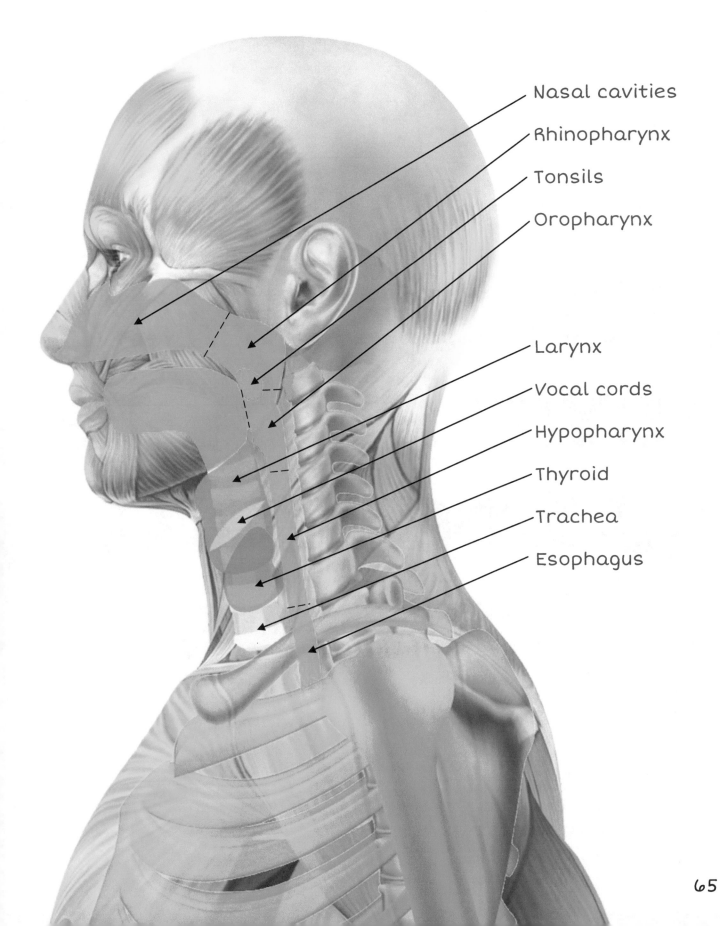

Nasal cavities

Rhinopharynx

Tonsils

Oropharynx

Larynx

Vocal cords

Hypopharynx

Thyroid

Trachea

Esophagus

THE DIGESTIVE SYSTEM AND ABDOMINAL ORGANS

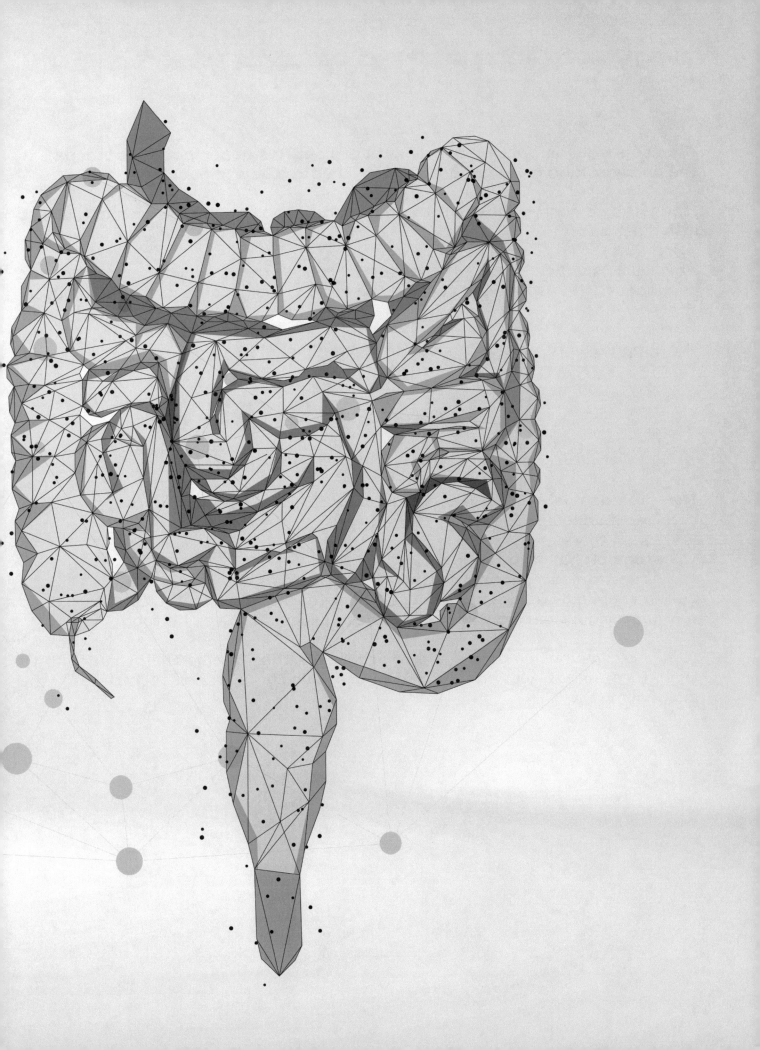

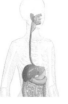

THE ESOPHAGUS

The esophagus is part of the digestive tract. Its upper part is attached to the pharynx, and its lower part is attached to the stomach.

Its role is to carry food from the mouth and pharynx to the stomach where it is digested.

When we swallow food, it passes through the pharynx and into the esophagus. The esophagus carries the food to our stomach through muscle contractions.

The esophagus of an adult is about 30 cm (11 inch) long.

THE STOMACH

The stomach is a sac-like organ located just below the esophagus. It receives swallowed food. Its role is to ensure the digestion of food.

The stomach has two functions:
- A mechanical function, because it mixes and stirs the food.
- A chemical function, because it produces chemical elements called gastric juices (or gastric acid). These juices dissolve the food.

It is the combination of these two processes that allows the stomach (1) to transform what we eat into a mush, which is then poured into the duodenum (2).

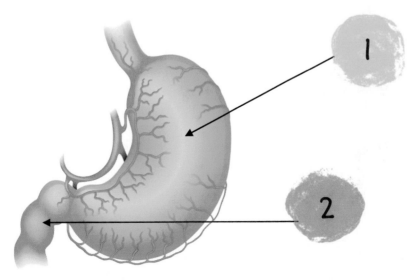

Depending on what we eat, digestion in the stomach takes between 3 and 7 hours.

The gastric juices are very acidic. The inside of the stomach is protected by a thick mucus. Without this protection, the stomach could digest itself.

THE PANCREAS

The pancreas is an organ located behind the stomach.

It has two main functions:
- The pancreas secretes and releases pancreatic juices that are released into the duodenum (the upper part of the small intestine) and are involved in the digestion of fats.
- The pancreas helps maintain blood sugar levels (Blood sugar is the amount of sugar, also called glucose, in the blood). The pancreas secretes hormones (including insulin), which help store glucose in the liver and muscles. This stored glucose is an energy reserve for our body.

THE LIVER

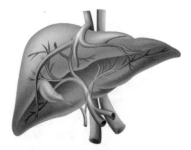

The liver is an organ of the digestive system.

It is located in the right part of the abdomen and is partly protected by the ribs.

The liver is divided into four lobes of unequal size. The largest lobe is the hepatic lobe. The gallbladder is attached to the liver.

The gallbladder is a small hollow organ (like a small bag). Its main function is to store bile.

This bile is a liquid produced by the liver and is necessary for digestion, especially after a heavy meal.

The liver has several functions:
- Maintaining blood sugar: After digestion, glycogen (made up of several types of carbohydrate molecules) is stored in the liver. When blood sugar levels drop, the liver stabilizes blood sugar levels by breaking down glycogen.
- Protein synthesis: The liver synthesizes cholesterol (we are talking about the "good" cholesterol, also called HDL - High Density Lipoprotein). This good cholesterol helps clean the body of bad cholesterol, capturing it and transporting it to the liver for elimination. Cholesterol is a fatty substance produced by the liver, but also comes from food. The liver also produces many other substances, such as albumin (a protein that makes up blood plasma), and other proteins related to blood.
- Elimination of waste : The liver removes many of the toxic substances from the body. For example, the liver eliminates ammonia, which is a substance produced during digestion (in the colon) but which is toxic to our brain. This ammonia is transformed into urea and eliminated in the urine. The liver also allows the elimination of alcohol, or certain medicinal substances. Finally, the liver allows the elimination of red blood cells, which are destroyed in the spleen. During this process, a toxic substance, yellow in color, is released. The liver then eliminates this substance through the bladder (which gives the color to our urine).
- The digestive function: The liver (1) produces bile, a yellow substance that mainly allows the digestion of fats. The bile is then stored in the gallbladder (2).

THE SPLEEN

The spleen is a small organ located under the diaphragm, to the left of the stomach. The spleen stores lymphocytes, which are the body's protective cells. In case of infection, the spleen releases millions of immune cells into the bloodstream to fight viruses or bacteria.

The spleen also produces blood cells, like bone marrow.

Finally, the spleen helps to eliminate "spent" red blood cells by destroying them. The residue is then eliminated in the urine.

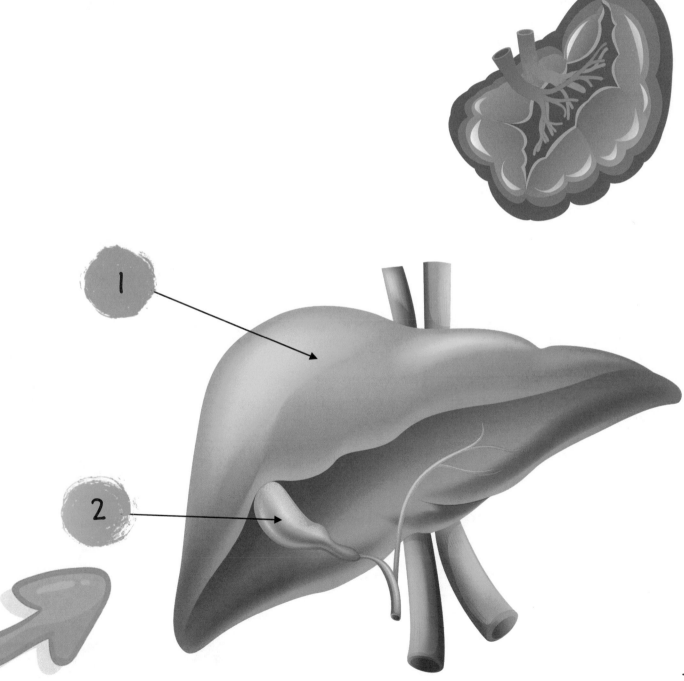

THE SMALL INTESTINE

The small intestine is the longest part of the digestive tract. It is about 7 meters long (23 ft).
The role of the small intestine is to absorb nutrients from digestion.
The inside of the small intestine is lined with villi (which look like tiny tentacles). These villi allow the different nutrients (proteins, fats, carbohydrates...) to pass into the bloodstream.

The small intestine is composed of 3 parts:

- The duodenum: This is the upper part of the small intestine, which communicates directly with the stomach. When the food digested by the stomach arrives in the duodenum, it is mixed with new gastric juices from the liver (bile juices) and the pancreas (pancreatic juices).
- The jejunum and the ileum: These two successive parts represent the major part of the small intestine. It is in these parts that the majority of nutrients (proteins, lipids, carbohydrates, electrolytes, vitamins...) will be absorbed by the villi and pass into the blood. The small intestine also absorbs part of the water contained in the food.

THE COLON

The colon, also called large intestine, is located in the continuity of the small intestine. It measures about 1.5 meters (5 ft).

The digestible substances (therefore absorbable by our body) have been collected by the small intestine. The indigestible substances (not absorbable) and the water residue are directed towards the colon.
The colon will then recover the water and compact the non-digested substances. This is how stool (also called fecal matter) is formed. This fecal matter will be evacuated into the rectum.

The appendix is located in the colon. This small growth contains immune cells.

The colon is populated by a multitude of bacteria called the intestinal flora, which has a very important role in the digestion process.

THE INTESTINAL FLORA

The intestinal flora is the set of bacteria that mainly inhabit our colon, but also the terminal part of the small intestine.
This flora colonizes our intestine from the first days of our life. It is essential to our organism.

The intestinal flora is composed of about 10,000 billion bacteria, of 400 different species.

The intestinal flora has several roles:
- It helps digestion by breaking down the amino acids present in undigested matter. This decomposition produces gas that is more or less important depending on the food.
- It participates in the proper functioning of the immune system by protecting the digestive tract from potentially dangerous bacteria.
- It participates in the synthesis of certain vitamins (B5, B8, B12 and K for example).

THE RECTUM AND THE ANUS

The rectum is the last part of the digestive tract. It is located in the pelvis (between the hips). Its role is to store fecal matter before it is evacuated through the anus.

The anus is the terminal orifice of the digestive tract. Its function is simply to evacuate the feces (fecal matter).

Colon

Small intestine

Appendix

Rectum

Anus

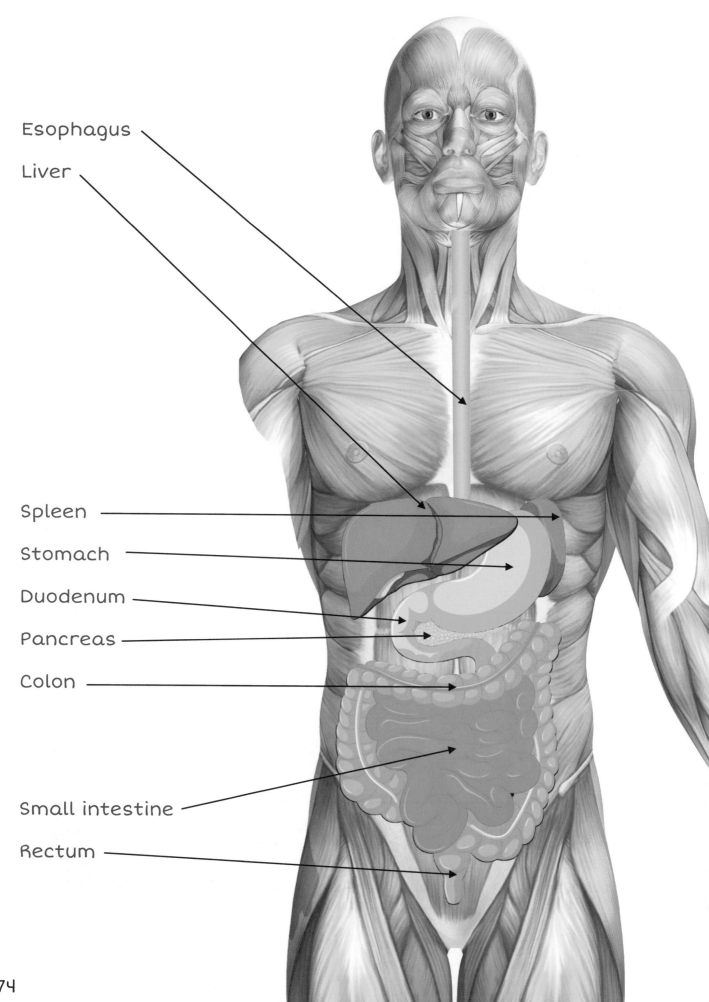

Esophagus

Liver

Spleen

Stomach

Duodenum

Pancreas

Colon

Small intestine

Rectum

74

The liver is the largest abdominal organ in the human body. The liver is able to regenerate quickly after an injury or partial surgical removal.

Our feces are normally brown in color. This color comes from the pigments in the bile (which is produced by the liver).

The intestines are sometimes called the second brain, because of their very large number of neurons.
Recent scientific studies have shown that there is a very important link between the intestines and the brain. For example, it has been shown that an imbalance in the intestines can lead to psychological disorders (such as stress or depression). Finally, some scientists are studying the possible link between intestinal balance and certain neurodegenerative diseases, such as Parkinson's or Alzheimer's.)

THE URINARY SYSTEM

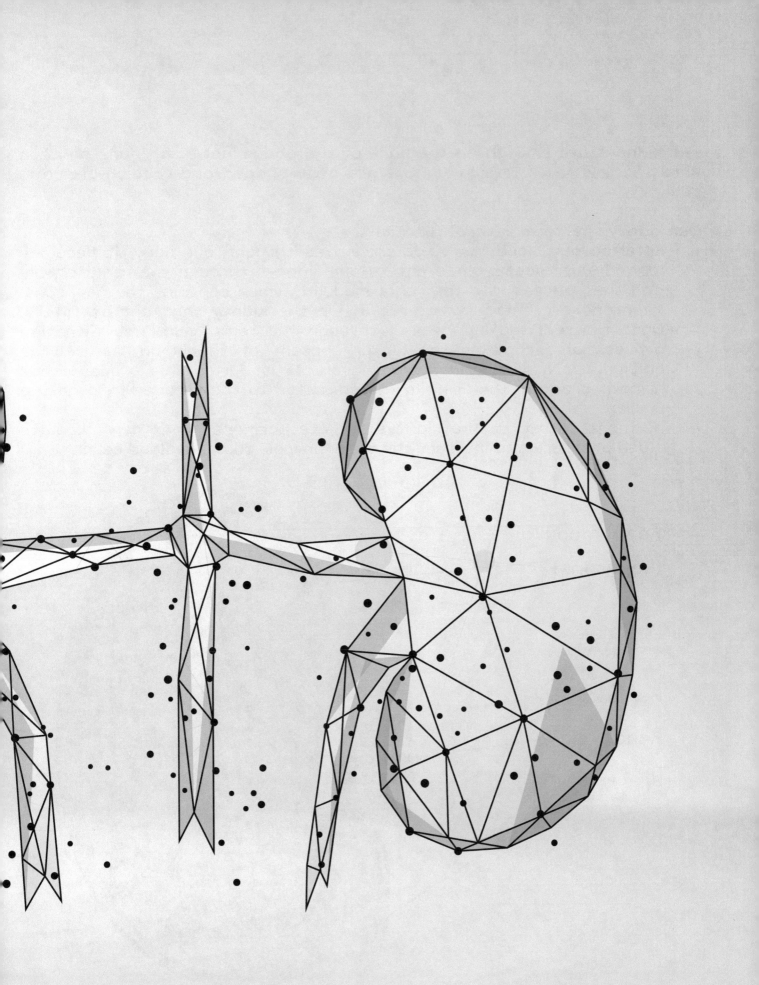

THE KIDNEYS

The kidneys are located on the back of the abdominal cavity, one on each side of the spine. Our two kidneys are bean-shaped and reddish-brown in color.

Our kidneys perform several functions:

- Filtering our blood: As blood circulates through our body, it becomes loaded with waste. Blood enters our kidneys through the renal artery and then passes into the renal medulla, which contains the nephrons. Nephrons are small structures inside the kidney that act as filters. Once filtered, the blood exits through the renal vein. This filtration process also controls the water content of the blood, as well as calcium, potassium and sodium levels. It is during this process that urine is created. The urine is then directed to the bladder through the ureter.
- Hormone secretion: The kidneys secrete hormones that help regulate blood pressure and instruct the bone marrow to make blood cells.

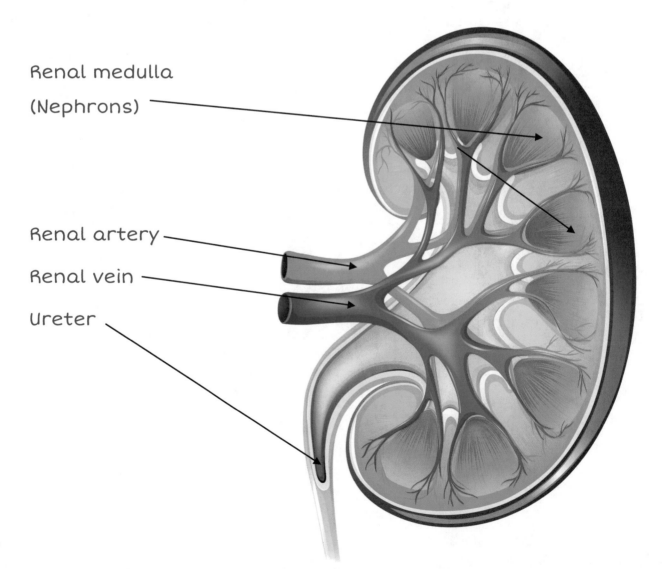

Renal medulla

(Nephrons)

Renal artery

Renal vein

Ureter

THE REPRODUCTIVE SYSTEM

THE BLADDER AND THE URETHRA

The bladder is a pouch designed to store the urine produced by the kidneys. Once full, it empties through the urethra.

The urethra is a channel (a pipe) that connects the bladder to the tip of the penis (for men) and the vulva (for women). It is simply used to pass urine. In men, the urethra is also where the sperm comes out.

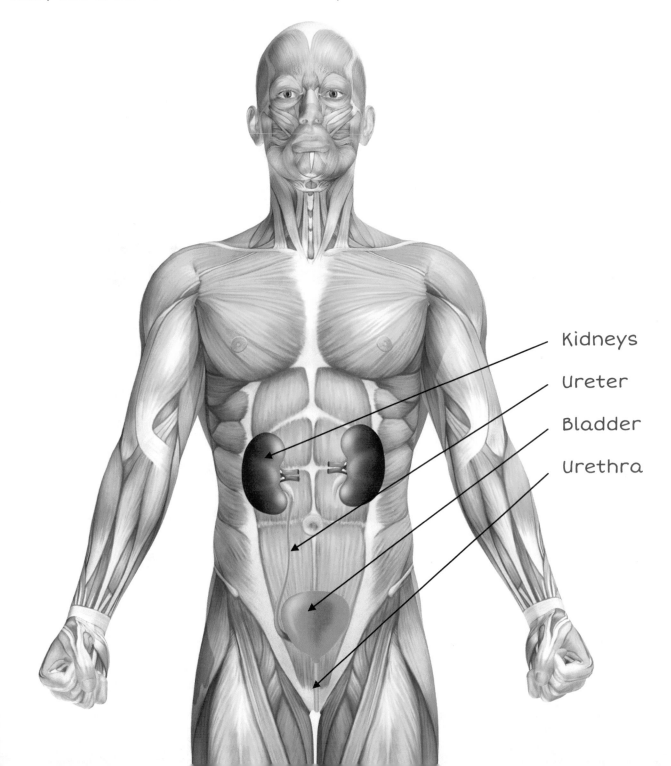

Kidneys

Ureter

Bladder

Urethra

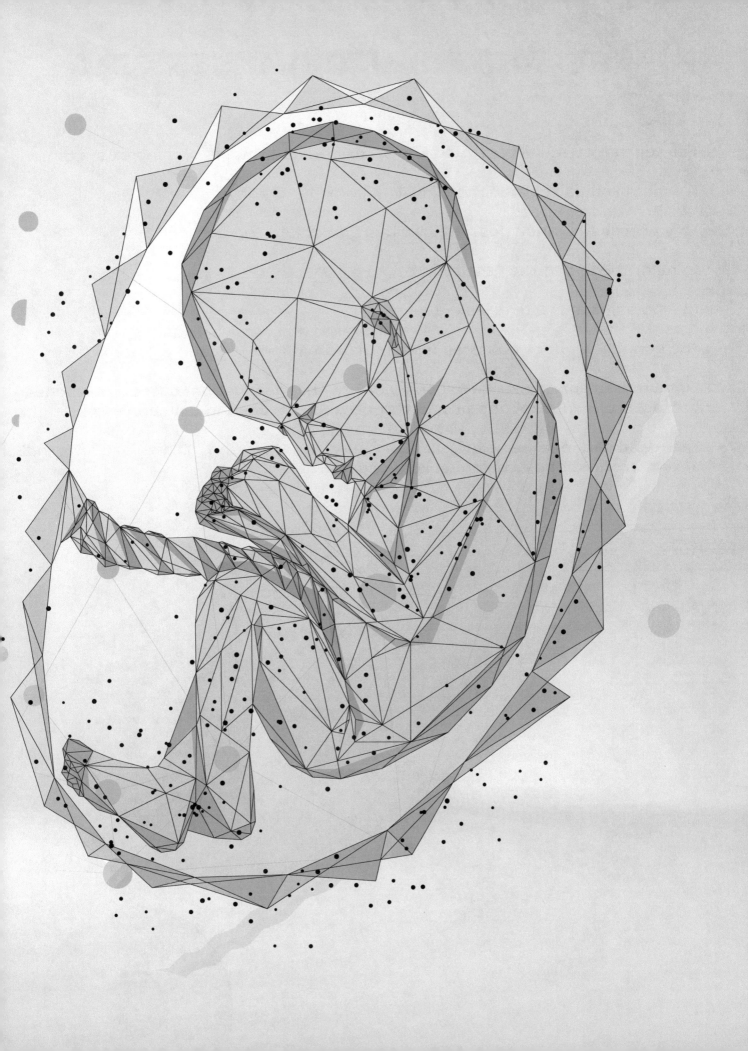

THE REPRODUCTIVE SYSTEM

The reproductive system, also known as the genitals, is a complex system.

Its main role is reproduction, that is "making" a baby.

This process is made possible by an organ called the gonad.

In men, these are the testicles.

In women, it is the ovaries.

The gonads produce gametes (spermatozoa in men, eggs in women).

Finally, the gonads are responsible for the production of sex hormones: testosterone in men, and progesterone and estrogen in women.

The genitalia are very different in men and women. There are internal sexual organs, and external sexual organs.

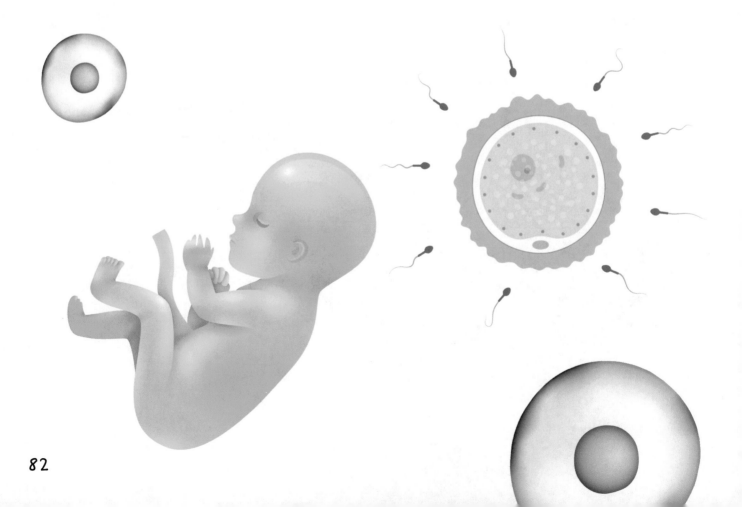

THE MALE REPRODUCTIVE SYSTEM

Penis: The penis is an organ that can swell and harden with a blood supply. This process is called erection, and allows for sexual intercourse (or penetration). It is during this sexual intercourse that the sperm, containing the spermatozoa, will be released into the vagina (female sexual organ) and allow fertilization. The penis is crossed by the urethra.

The glans: The glans is the end of the penis. It is crossed by a great number of nerve endings and is covered by a skin called the foreskin.

Scrotum: The scrotum, also called the bursa, is the skin that protects the testicles.

The testicles: The two testicles are located in the scrotum, and are ovoid in shape. It is in the testicles that the spermatozoa are made: First, stem cells are produced. Under the action of hormones, these cells will transform and become spermatozoa. A healthy adult male produces between 100 and 200 million spermatozoa every day.

The prostate gland: The prostate is an internal gland whose function is the production of seminal fluid (i.e. the fluid containing the spermatozoa). The prostate also serves to seal off the urethra during ejaculation, preventing semen from mixing with urine.

The seminal vesicles: The two seminal vesicles are located right next to the prostate. They also produce seminal fluid and participate in the ejaculation process by contracting.

Bladder
Seminal vesicles
Prostate
Urethra
Penis
Testicles
Glans
Scrotum

THE FEMALE REPRODUCTIVE SYSTEM

Vulva: The vulva is the external part of the female genitalia. It is formed by the labia majora and minora, which protect the entrance to the vagina. The urethra also opens at the vulva.

Clitoris: The clitoris is a small organ with many nerve endings.

The vagina: The vagina is a duct that starts at the vulva and ends at the uterus. The main function of the vagina is to receive the penis during sexual intercourse. It also serves as a passage for the flow of blood during menstruation. Finally, it is through the vagina that the baby comes out during childbirth.

The uterus: The uterus is a hollow organ intended for gestation, i.e. the development of a baby in the maternal belly. It is lined with a mucous membrane that allows blood exchanges between the fetus (the future baby) and the mother. And when there is no fetus, this mucous membrane gets rid of the excess blood: This is the menstruation. The uterus is connected to the vagina by the cervix.

Fallopian tubes: The two fallopian tubes are located on each side of the uterus. They connect the uterus to the ovaries.

Ovaries: The ovaries are the female reproductive organs (like the testicles in men). The ovaries produce eggs. Unlike men, who produce millions of sperm every day, the ovaries usually produce only one egg per cycle (a cycle lasts about 28 days). The egg will then be taken to the fallopian tube (it is in the fallopian tube that the meeting and fertilization with the sperm will take place). The fertilized egg will then be taken to the uterus where it will attach itself and begin its development process. If the egg is not fertilized, then it dies and disappears.

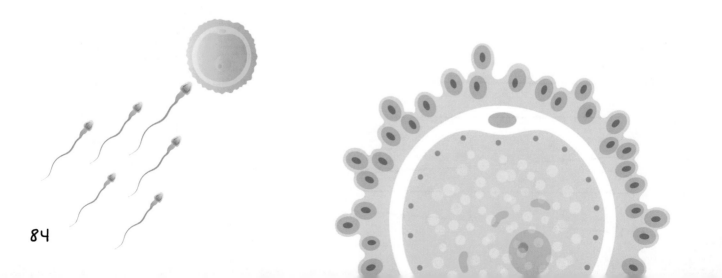

Fallopian tubes

Ovaries

Uterus

Cervix

Vagina

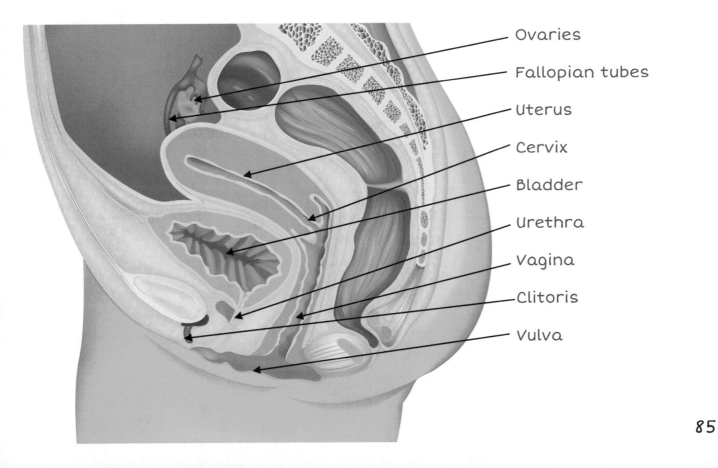

Ovaries

Fallopian tubes

Uterus

Cervix

Bladder

Urethra

Vagina

Clitoris

Vulva

THE BREASTS

The breasts are located in the thorax, in front of the pectoral muscle. They are supported by ligaments, and do not contain muscles.

The function of the breasts is to suckle newborns. The phenomenon of milk production is called lactation.

The breasts are made up of :
- The mammary gland, consisting of 15 to 25 lobes that contain lobules. These lobules produce breast milk. The milk is then transported to the nipple through small ducts (only when the baby is suckling).
- The areola, which is a pigmented area of skin that surrounds the nipple.
- The nipple, which functions as a nipple and allows milk to flow out.
- The breast is also made up of fatty tissue. It is this tissue that gives the breast its shape and volume.

Lactation is a phenomenon that occurs after childbirth, under the effect of several hormones. When the baby sucks, and under the effect of sucking on the nipple, other hormones cause lactation again, and so on.

The breasts appear at the time of puberty: Under the influence of hormones (estrogen and progesterone), the mammary gland will develop and the breasts will increase in volume, as well as the areola and the nipple.

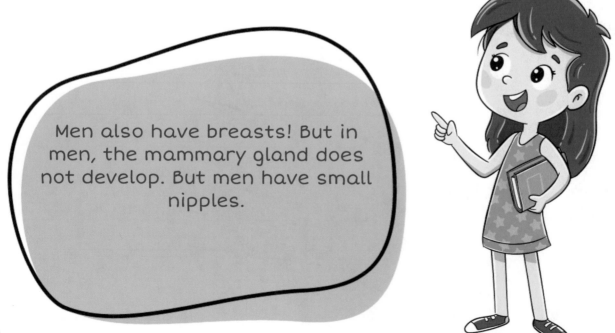

Men also have breasts! But in men, the mammary gland does not develop. But men have small nipples.

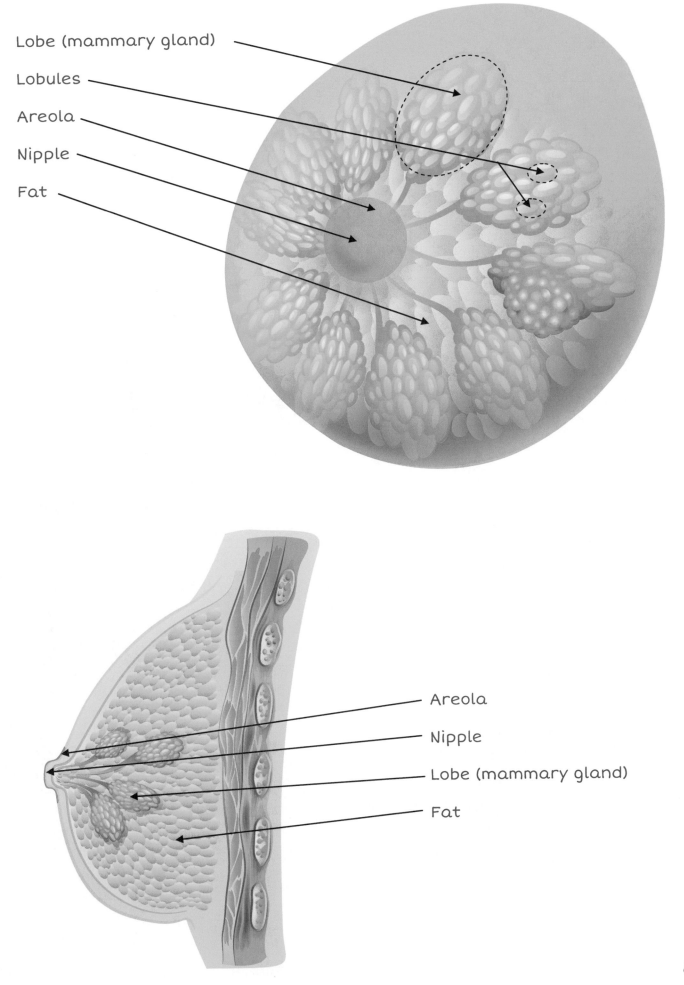

Lobe (mammary gland)

Lobules

Areola

Nipple

Fat

Areola

Nipple

Lobe (mammary gland)

Fat

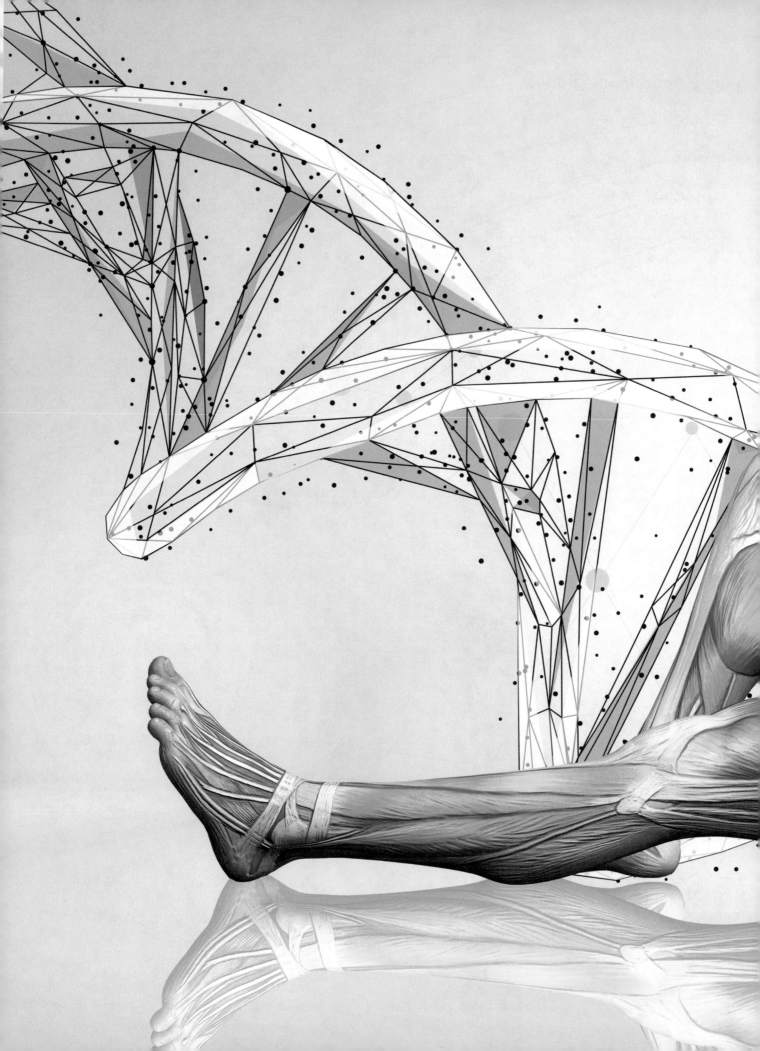

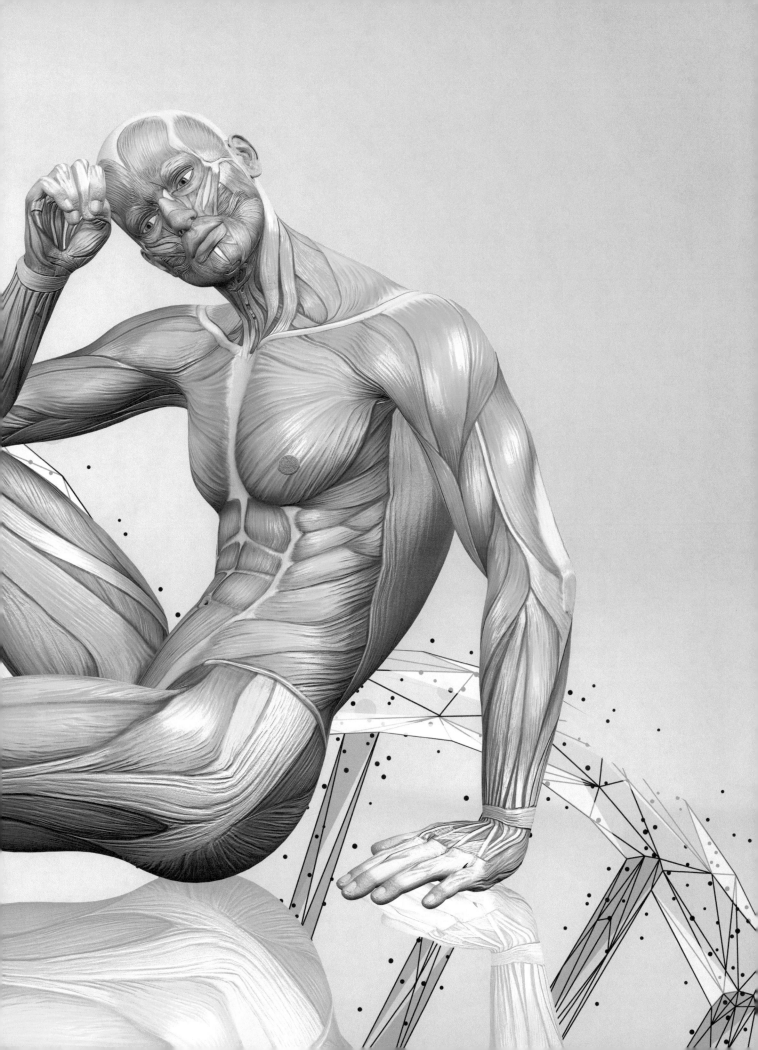

Made in the USA
Columbia, SC
27 February 2024

32259776R00050